D1416640

Cornel West

Cornel West

John Morrison

CHELSEA HOUSE
PUBLISHERS

A Haights Cross Communications Company

Philadelphia

CHELSEA HOUSE PUBLISHERS

VP, NEW PRODUCT DEVELOPMENT Sally Cheney
DIRECTOR OF PRODUCTION Kim Shinners
CREATIVE MANAGER Takeshi Takahashi
MANUFACTURING MANAGER Diann Grasse

Staff for CORNEL WEST

EDITOR Sally Cheney
EDITORIAL ASSISTANT Josh Spiegel
PRODUCTION ASSISTANT Megan Emery
ASSISTANT PHOTO EDITOR Noelle Nardone
SERIES & COVER DESIGNER Terry Mallon
LAYOUT Jennifer Krassy Peiler

A Haights Cross Communications ✦ Company

www.chelseahouse.com

First Printing

36242060339500

1 3 5 7 9 8 6 4 2

Library of Congress Cataloging-in-Publication Data applied for

ISBN 0-7910-7686-5

Table of Contents

INTRODUCTION

Beginning with the publication of the series *Black Americans of Achievement* nearly twenty years ago, Chelsea House Publishers made a commitment to publishing biographies for young adults that celebrated the lives of many of the country's most outstanding African Americans. The mix of individuals whose lives we covered was eclectic, to say the least. Some were well known—Dr. Martin Luther King, Jr., for example—although others we covered might be lesser known—Madam C.J. Walker, for example. Some—like the actor Danny Glover—were celebrities with legions of adoring fans. It mattered not what an individual's "star" quality might be, or how well known they were to the general public. What mattered was the life of the individual— their actions, their deeds, and, ultimately, their influence on the lives of others and our nation, as a whole. By telling the life stories of these unique Americans, we hoped to tell the story of how ordinary individuals are transformed by extraordinary circumstances to people of greatness. We hoped that the special lives we covered would inspire and encourage our young-adult readers to go out in the world and make a positive difference; and judging from the many wonderful letters that we have received over the years from students, librarians, and teachers about our *Black Americans of Achievement* biographies, we are certain that many of our readers did just that!

Now, some twenty years later, we are proud to release this new series of biographies, *African-American Leaders,* which we hope will make a similar mark on the lives of our young-adult readers. The individuals whose lives we cover in this first set of six books are all contemporary

African-American leaders. As these individuals are all living, the biographers made every attempt to interview their subjects so they could provide first-hand accounts and interesting anecdotes about each subject's life.

After reading about the likes of Henry Louis Gates, Jr., Cornel West, Condoleezza Rice, Carol Moseley-Braun, Eleanor Holmes Norton, and Benjamin Hooks, we think you will agree that the lives of these African-American leaders are remarkable. By overcoming the barriers that racism placed in their paths, they are an example of the power and resiliency of the human spirit and an inspiration to us all.

The Editor
Chelsea House Publishers

1

Man in a Hurry

> "Black people in the United States differ from all other modern people owing to the unprecedented levels of unregulated and unrestrained violence against them. No other people have been taught systematically to hate themselves—psychic violence—reinforced by the powers of state and civic coercion—physical violence—for the primary purpose of controlling their minds and exploiting their labor for nearly 400 years."
>
> —Cornel West, *Race Matters*

It was 1966, and Cornel West was 13 years old. He was a student at the new John F. Kennedy High School in Sacramento, California. He was on the track team, and his coach decided he wanted to teach him to swim.

The coach, who was white, took young Cornel out of the all-black neighborhood that he so loved – where he felt comfortable. Cornel's coach brought him to the white section of town where young Cornel was an unwelcome outsider. The coach lived in a "whites only" apartment complex (i.e., housing that discriminated against blacks), that had a pool in which the coach intended to teach Cornel to swim.

On the day of the lesson, there were swimmers in the pool—all white, of course. When Cornel and the coach jumped into the water, the white swimmers leaped from the pool as if a hungry shark had just shown its fin in the water.

Later, the pool was drained.

In an interview more than 30 years later, West appeared to remain in a state of shock over the incident.

"I polluted the pool!" he said in wonder. "I contaminated it! I thought, 'What is going on? What is wrong with me?' It hit me on a deep level."

"The apartment manager told the coach, 'Don't ever bring that little so-and-so here again.' The coach was so upset. He didn't know what to do. He was a very progressive white brother." He later moved out of the complex in protest.

It was not that West was unaware of racism; he just had not experienced it in such a harsh manner before.

The shocking event at the white pool was not to be the last racist incident to afflict a man whom many consider one of the most outstanding scholars, teachers, and writers in the fields of philosophy, theology, and African-American studies. West has been stopped by the police, called racist names, sent death threats, and once as he stood on a street corner in New York City in a hurry to keep an appointment, looked on in amazement as nine taxis rolled by, refusing to stop and pick him up. Once, his wife was even threatened with a gun.

He admits to seething with anger over these incidents. Yet, through it all, he has never deviated from his convictions about the best way to cope with racism in America. He believes the best way to touch the hearts and souls of

This picture of the John F. Kennedy High School's 1969 cross-country track team includes the young Cornel West (seated second row, one from left). West's experiences confronting racism, beginning in his youth, reaffirmed his belief that real social change is achieved only through organized and compassionate political pressure.

the desperate people living marginal lives in terrible circumstances, and the best way to effect change in the nation's political system, is through pressure applied with love, compassion, and, equally important, organization.

West now teaches philosophy, religion, and African-American courses at Princeton University. He previously taught at Harvard University, Yale University, Union Theological Seminary, and other major institutions of higher learning. He has written 16 books and numerous articles. His ninth book, *Race Matters*, published in 1993 by Vintage Books, was his most accessible and certainly his most popular to date. It sold nearly half a million copies. In addition, many books and articles have been written about West. Learned thinkers of many disciplines have commented on his work.

SINGING THE BLUES

Although his base of operations has always been the lofty spaces of the academia, West knows how to talk to ordinary folk. In fact, that is what he enjoys doing the most—venturing from the halls of academia to the streets, barbershops, churches, mosques, nightclubs, schools, and prisons of America's cities. He lectures to a wide variety of audiences about 150 times a year—an exceptionally heavy schedule for a scholar.

West knows how to talk to young people, too, including those trapped in the hopelessness and despair of the drug-infested inner cities. He knows what to say to prisoners to give them hope. He has stacks of mail on the desk of his office at Princeton University from youngsters and prison inmates who tell him he has shown them the kind of future they dared not dream of before.

West's idols are not only the major philosophers, theologians, and writers of history, but jazz artists, blues singers, and rappers. He cites as major influences in his life people like John Coltrane, Louis Armstrong, Charlie Parker, Marvin Gaye, Billie Holiday, and Sarah Vaughan. He sees jazz and the blues as perhaps the best vehicles for describing the plight of black people in America. Yet, at the same time, he sees the two musical genres as great sources of inspiration and hope.

Blues songs tell the sad stories of lost loves, scheming women (and men), fallen-down shacks, jailhouses, tobacco fields, and the lure of drink and drugs. But they also possess a spirit and drive that keeps hope alive, holding out the promise of better days to come.

West has drawn on the power of music by recording a spoken-word CD—a kind of "intellectual rap"—that he hopes will convey his positive message to young people who would rather listen to music than read books. Some of his fellow academics severely criticized him for doing so, saying that such a project demeans West's stature as a first-rate teacher and scholar.

He has also received criticism for some of his political activities, especially those associated with the presidential campaigns of Green Party candidate Ralph Nader and Reverend Al Sharpton, a controversial figure from New York City. A famous dispute with the president of Harvard University over these and other issues led to West's resignation as a professor there in 2002. It was a clash that made headlines, and page-one stories in the *New York Times* and other news outlets.

West's participation in various demonstrations, which have led to clashes with the police, have also had some in the academic community concerned about him. But he says he has now found understanding and approval for his activism from the administration at Princeton University.

He travels all over the country for rallies, demonstrations, and protests, and appears frequently on radio and television panel discussions and interview shows. He tries to ignore the hate mail and death threats that come pouring in after his every appearance, a reminder to him and, perhaps to us all, that racism is not dead in America.

An obvious fact about Cornel West to all who see him clearly is that he truly loves his fellow human beings—so much so that he calls everybody "brother" and "sister." The

Over the years, West has taken many controversial stands—among them, his decision to support Green Party candidate Ralph Nader in the 2000 presidential election.

affection that those names imply is heartfelt. He even refers to President George W. Bush as "Brother Bush." He gives you a big hug when you leave him, and you get a sincere "God bless you" to take with you.

West believes people of all races, colors, and creeds face the same basic problems in America. They must discover how to succeed in a country that has not always kept its promises to its most needy citizens; how to face death, despair, loneliness, and fear; how to search for meaning; and how to find an identity and self-worth against the odds.

West is especially concerned about young people growing up without the kind of love and concern with which he grew up. He tries to convince them that there are better ways of dealing with their situation than drugs, sex, violence, and crime. He tells them, and shows by example, that they can redirect their anger to more constructive pursuits.

West has a special place in his heart for the under-dogs and outcasts of American society, including gays and lesbians. He speaks out against the tendencies of some black leaders and black churches to condemn these people in the name of religion. He also opposes anti-Semitism (discrimination against Jewish people), which exists in some black communities despite the fact that many Jews worked hard for civil rights over the years and even gave up their lives in the struggle for racial justice. Among his heroes are Dr. Martin Luther King, Jr., W.E.B. Du Bois, and Malcom X. He sees himself upholding the non-violent and compassionate traditions of Dr. King and Mahatma Gandhi (India's best-known champion of civil rights).

West has worked with the Black Panthers (a political organization dedicated to helping African Americans) in their prison outreach programs. He frequently speaks at Sunday morning services at black churches, although he is not an ordained minister. Just to show how much he gets around, he even agreed to take on a role in the sequels to the popular film *The Matrix*.

West is an amazing scholar. He seems to have read the major works of nearly all of the most influential thinkers throughout history. Among the people he cites as major influences on his early thinking—even as a teenager-—are the Greek philosopher Socrates, the Russian author Anton Chekhov, the Danish philosopher Søren Kierkegaard, and Jesus Christ. He reads Hebrew, Aramaic, and Koine Greek—the original languages of the Judaic-Christian Bible.

West graduated with honors from Harvard University at the age of 19, received his master's degree at 20, and his doctorate from Princeton University at the age of 24, while teaching at Union Theological Seminary in New York!

Someone at Princeton University once remarked to him, "You know, Cornel, you really seem to be in a hurry."

THE UNFINISHED SOCIETY

Cornel West is basically a teacher. But his teaching extends beyond the halls of academia. He wants his message of love, understanding, and above all, hope to reach deep into all the dark corners of society and bring light into the shadows.

West has never allowed himself to give in to hopelessness. He views American democracy as an unfinished work. He looks at history and sees the many changes that have occurred, changes that have bettered the lives of citizens of all colors and creeds. Moreover, he believes that change will continue—even in the face of stubborn obstacles.

For blacks, the barriers against attaining the "American dream" of liberty and equality for all have historically been racism and white supremacy—a long and bitter legacy dating to their arrival in America as slaves. For later generations, these horrors continued with Jim Crow, the Ku Klux Klan, and lynch mobs.

Today, racism is more subtle and harder to detect in many parts of the country. West admits that much progress has been made to bring blacks into the mainstream. Still, there are those who are left behind—and they are the ones who touch his heart.

West sees America's market economy, with its televised promises of the "good life" to all who buy the products advertised, as part of the problem. He believes such images, sent into even the poorest homes, lead to a yearning, especially among young people, for instant gratification. Lost in the frantic rush for pleasure and material possessions are the old virtues of patience, spirituality, caring, and love.

People of all races and colors are affected. But in some black communities, where attaining the good life offered by the TV merchants is tragically remote, West believes that too many young people turn to the instant excitement of drugs, sex, violence, and crime.

With the loss of values and a spiritual foundation come feelings of worthlessness and self-hate. Among the silent victims of this anguish are black women, who, West believes, bear a large brunt of the anger that comes from the frustrated black men in their communities. This deeply saddens West and other black leaders.

Throughout history, African Americans have turned to many causes and movements in desperate efforts to build a better life. The black church has always been an institution that offered comfort, meaning, and a sense of self-worth to its members. There have also been more radical solutions, including Marcus Garvey's "back to Africa" movement of the 1920s. Garvey's movement captured the imaginations of many blacks who had concluded that America was a hopeless case, and a return to the homeland might be the answer. About 100 years earlier, former American slaves had founded the West African country of Liberia.

Then there was black nationalism in the 1960s and 1970s, which was often accompanied by an aggressive anti-white character. It led in extreme cases to calls for revolution and violence. The early Black Muslims, founded by Elijah

Muhammad, were a black nationalist religion. Elijah Muhammad's followers turned to Islam after reaching the conclusion that Christianity was no longer working for the black underclass.

Then came Martin Luther King, Jr. with a new idea: confront the white establishment with demands for change—but with a non-violent approach. King preached the power of civil disobedience—deliberately violating laws considered unjust and racist, without the use of violence—to effect change. He told his followers never to meet violence with violence. It was the method Gandhi used to force the British out of India. (Gandhi, in fact, was a strong influence on King.)

Cornel West was two years old in December 1955 when a black woman named Rosa Parks refused to give up her seat on a bus to a white person—as required by law—in Montgomery, Alabama. Her arrest led to a bus boycott by blacks, directed by Martin Luther King, Jr. Most blacks refused to ride on the city buses from December 5, 1955, to December 20, 1956, devastating the local economy. Finally, the United States Supreme Court threw out the segregation law and forced the integration of the buses.

African Americans had won a great victory, and the only violence that came with it was strictly on the side of the segregationists. Dr. King went on to lead demonstrations and marches for black voting rights and an end to Jim Crow laws that kept blacks segregated, poor, and powerless. King was jailed in Birmingham, Alabama, in 1963, and wrote his famous "Letter From Birmingham Jail," calling for white preachers to join the fight. A year later, he received the Nobel Peace Prize.

Some of the freedom fighters who braved police dogs, cattle prods, and fire hoses, gave up their lives for the cause of freedom and justice, including King. Tragically, King was shot and killed on April 4, 1968, in Memphis, Tennessee, while fighting for the rights of garbage and trash collectors.

West will continue to do battle in the name of the many causes about which he feels passionate—affirmative action, racial profiling by police, police brutality, poor housing, bad schools, and unemployment. He has also taken on international issues, such as the Israeli-Palestinian conflict.

And he does so with his strong commitment to the Christian principles of love, compassion, and understanding—even for one's enemies.

THE MAN IN THE BLACK SUIT

West's office on the Princeton University campus is in a massive stone building that looks as if it had been built to hold off an army rather than to house faculty members. It is called 1879 Hall—for the date of its construction.

Founded in 1746 as the College of New Jersey, Princeton University is one of the most prestigious and academically rigorous universities in the country. (West's previous employer, Harvard University, is even older, founded in 1636!)

Princeton University, and the other schools of its stature, have a long tradition of excellence in education. They are home to scholars and thinkers who ponder the problems of life, people, and nations.

When you first enter West's office, you are struck by one impressive sight—the books. Books are stacked neatly on shelves along every wall, from floor to ceiling. The only spaces that don't have books are the door and the window. It's clear that West is a man who loves books. It looks as if every scholar who ever had a deep thought and wrote about it is represented here. But there is also a biography of the jazz saxophonist John Coltrane, and books about other musicians, civil rights leaders, educators, and more. After a conversation with the bearded black man behind the desk, one could easily believe that he just might have read every one of those books.

The next impressive thing about West's office is West himself. He is a man of coiled energy. He moves restlessly back and forth in his chair, his delicate fingers interlaced, his voice a conspiratorial whisper to make a point, now rearing back with laughter at something that tickled him. He jumps up frequently to grab a book off a shelf to find a favorite passage. His books are a mess of underlining and margin notations. He is dressed in a black suit—much like a preacher would wear—with a scarf around his neck to protect the voice he relies on to communicate his ideas. His thick mustache and goatee are flecked with gray and his spectacles give him a scholarly look.

Outside on Princeton's tree-lined campus there is a 5-degree wind-chill factor, but West walks to a favorite restaurant without a coat. "I've never worn a coat," he says. A California native, West doesn't seem inclined to give in to Northern weather.

He lunches on his favorite, veal parmesan, at the Annex, a restaurant on Princeton's main drag. He greets all acquaintances with a big, friendly hello and a hug. He once told journalist and interviewer Bill Moyers that one of his aims is to "let suffering speak, let victims be visible, and let social misery be put on the agenda of those in power." A tall order for a man who also once wrote, "I'm just trying to make some sense of the world, and love folks before I die."

2

The Making
of a Scholar

> "So much of my life was spent where I didn't interact
> with white brothers and sisters at all. And I think, in the
> end, that was a very positive thing, because it gave me a
> chance to really revel in black humanity, and when it
> became time to interact with white brothers and sisters,
> I could really see them just as humans. I didn't have to
> either deify them or demonize them; I didn't have to put
> them on a pedestal or put them in the gutter."
> —Cornel West, *The Cornel West Reader*

Cornel West was born in Tulsa, Oklahoma, on June 2, 1953. When he was four years old, the family moved to a segregated section of Sacramento, California, called Glen Elder.

West cherishes his childhood memories. His parents, Clifton L. West, Jr. and Irene West, were loving and talented parents. His father, who died in 1994, was a civilian employee

Cornel West (seen standing at right in this family portrait) grew up in a segregated section of Sacramento during the 1960s. His father, Clifton West, Jr., was a civilian employee of the McClellan Air Force Base. His mother, Irene, was a schoolteacher and principal. West remains close with his brother Clifton, III (standing, left), who was executive producer of Cornel's spoken-word album.

of the United States Air Force, working at McClellan Air Force Base in Sacramento. His mother was a schoolteacher and principal. She was so highly thought of in the city that an elementary school was named after her.

West expresses an almost hero-worship attitude toward his older brother, Clifton L. West III, who was a standout athlete at their high school. His brother was a distance runner on the track team and was good enough to go to the 1972 Olympics in Munich, Germany, as an alternate. West is still very close to his brother, who was in the computer software business and wrote music on the side. He was the executive producer of Cornel's spoken-word album.

"I've always believed that if I were one-half the person my brother is and one-third the person my mother and father were, I would actually be a high quality person," he said in an interview.

"Look at it from inside," he said, by way of explanation. "Tolstoy's son wrote fine short stories, but his father wrote *Anna Karenina*, he wrote *War and Peace*. When you have that kind of standard, you have to look at what you're doing."

Reminded of his own accomplishments, he said, "I appreciate what people say about me. But my standards are so high in regard to the art of living."

West enjoys talking about his childhood. "It was a magnificent childhood," he said. "I had just unbelievable love. My mother and father provided unconditional love. It was the most fundamental experience of my life."

He said it was the combination of his parents' love and the Shiloh Baptist Church that shaped his early life. His grandfather, the Reverend C.L. West, was founder and pastor of the Metropolitan Baptist Church in Tulsa. West maintains a reverence for the way the black church provided love, hope, and support for black Christians through a long, and often bitter, history. West said he is sad when he sees young people who do not have the kind of upbringing he had.

"It [West's wonderful childhood] was totally undeserved," he said. "It just showed up in this particular family. I didn't ask for it, I'm not responsible for it. It just happened."

While it is true that the neighborhood he grew up in was segregated, it was still a positive place to grow up. In one interview West described Glen Elder as a tight-knit community in which most people were upbeat about the future.

"Even for black families with modest means in segregated neighborhoods, it was a land of pleasant single-family homes, of barbecues and baseball diamonds," he told Rosemary Cowan, author of *Cornel West: The Politics of Redemption*.

"All of us kids had dads, most with jobs—that we took for granted."

ANGRY YOUNG MAN

Despite the love of his family and the protection of the community and his church, West's early school years were marked by a sense of rage that he is hard-pressed to explain today.

"I was kind of the bad boy in class," he told Cowan. "I'd get in fights five or six times a week. I was full of energy and anger. I don't know where it came from, because my family was very loving."

He was expelled from school in the third grade for punching a pregnant teacher after she slapped him for refusing to salute the American flag. It is apparent that, even at an early age, Cornel sensed there was something wrong with a country that segregated blacks from whites— and where the white folk seemed to have the upper hand. He was aware, for example, that when his mother went shopping in a department store, the security guards kept a watch on her.

After his expulsion from school, no other school would have him, and for six months his mother taught him at home. He finally got into an "enrichment" school that was integrated. When he was 8 years old, West had a religious conversion that changed his attitude. He went on to excel in junior and senior high school. The bully in him was no longer in charge of his life. It might have been because of this that the incident at the all-white swimming pool did not send him into a murderous rage, as it might have if it had happened earlier.

It was also about this time that he decided he wanted to go to Harvard University. It was a strange ambition since he had no idea where Harvard was, or even what it was. The idea came to him after reading a biography of Theodore Roosevelt, the 26th president of the United States.

He discovered that Roosevelt had suffered from asthma, just as Cornel did in childhood. But Roosevelt overcame his sickness and went on to a great career as a soldier and statesman. Cornel also read that Roosevelt went to Harvard University. That was good enough for him. He would go to Harvard just like his hero.

Another influential childhood event occurred when West's coach convinced him to read *Uncle Tom's Cabin*, an antislavery novel by Harriet Beecher Stowe. He told his coach he was impressed by the love demonstrated by the novel's title character, Uncle Tom.

"He has the sense of love, no matter what," he told the coach. But the coach said, "People don't need to be bowing, they need to be standing up."

"I said, 'Well, I can agree with that, but I also think that people have to love no matter what, love through all the absurdity and darkness of the world.'"

In 1967, Cornel moved with his family to a white neighborhood of Sacramento. Before the move, a group of neighbors tried to buy the property to prevent them from moving in. In time, however, the West family was accepted by their white neighbors, and there were never any further problems.

At about the age of 10, West marched with his parents in a civil rights demonstration in Sacramento. His parents had their own personal experiences with the racial inequalities of the era. Both of West's parents had been born in Louisiana at a time when black people were kept powerless and afraid for their lives if they dared challenge the white establishment.

A LEADER AND SCHOLAR IS BORN

It wasn't until high school that the now young-adult Cornel began to emerge as the gifted leader and scholar that we know today.

At John F. Kennedy High School, Cornel became president of the student body. In that position, he found himself dealing with a sudden upsurge of violence between black and white students.

"The blacks were saying, 'Right on,' and the white kids thought they were saying, 'Riot on,'" he said.

The problems came after black kids started being bused into the school for integration purposes.

"I was student body president," he said. "I had to mediate. The white students thought they were being mistreated and the blacks thought they were being mistreated. We had some big, painful meetings."

"It was mostly a social thing," he said. "There was fighting in the halls. You always have a lunatic fringe. You had to isolate those thuggish elements and make sure they didn't speak on behalf of the rest of the students. You had to get some of the more decent folk involved, and that took courage. People were just scared. People were just downright scared."

While in high school, he and other black presidents of student bodies in other schools in the city decided to rally students to engage in a citywide strike to demand that the school district offer courses in black studies. "And we had good results," he wrote.

Girls Vice President
Shamin Khan

Boys' Vice President
Darold Ross

President: Cornel West

SPRING STUDENT GOVERNMENT

Secretary
Maureen Rule

Treasurer
Sallie Cochern

LEFT TO RIGHT: Bill Fong, Debbie Davis, Wayne Katsumata, Lou Anapolsky, Rick Delgado, Gary Kirk, Sue Hamilton, Kjersti Johnson, Leah Viegas, Maureen Rule, Dave Link, Sallie Cochern, Darold Ross, Tom Porter, Joane Palmi, Connie Reib, Pat Abbott, Debbie Barns, Jackie McAdams, Glenn Stephens, Shamin Khan, Liz Bell, Karen Erickson, Pat Whitten, Mike Castelle.

In high school, West distinguished himself as a well-rounded student—gifted in his academic pursuits, athletic prowess, and leadership qualities alike. In this picture we see a teenage West "hamming it up" for the camera as spring student government president.

His early introduction to the great thinkers of the world arrived on board a bookmobile that came regularly to his neighborhood.

"It was like a traveling library," he said. "I read every book in that bookmobile."

One of the books he read was by Søren Kierkegaard, the Danish philosopher. Kierkegaard, who lived from 1813 to 1855, was a gloomy guy. In fact, he is known as the "melancholy Dane." But something about his writings attracted the young Cornel West.

"He still remains to me one of the most profound thinkers of the modern world," he said.

It was reading Kierkegaard that got West interested in studying philosophy. He liked Kierkegaard's approach to religion. The philosopher was suspicious of people who claimed to know the truth, "with a capital T," as West put it.

"I loved that about him," West said. "He had a hunger for meaning."

Kierkegaard was aware of the limits of logic and reason in trying to understand the meaning of life and God.

"Pascal said that the heart has its reasons that reason knows not of," West said. (Blaise Pascal was a French scientist and religious philosopher. He lived from 1623 to 1662.) To West, this meant that the heart may know what the mind cannot grasp about spirituality.

Reading these thinkers at such a tender age led Cornel West to realize that his future would be in the study of philosophy (the search for the basic truths of life and the universe) and theology (the study of religion).

Another of the great experiences of his childhood was hearing Dr. Martin Luther King, Jr. speak. West was only 10 when his parents took him to the Memorial Auditorium in Sacramento.

"It was a magnificent moment," he said. "I didn't understand all he said, but he was so genuine, so sincere. You could see he was willing to live and die for what he talked about. I was so glad mom and dad took me there. He spoke from the soul."

Tragically, King was assassinated on April 4, 1968, two years before West graduated from high school.

"When Martin was killed, cities were going up in flames all over the country," he said.

It was then off to Harvard University, in Cambridge, Massachusetts, on a partial scholarship. To help pay his way, West had to take a job cleaning toilets.

"Harvard for me was tremendously liberating," he said. "It expanded my mind. I was exposed to a whole world of ideas. Reading, writing became my whole way of life. The teachers fundamentally changed my life. You've got to realize I'm coming from a public school, across the country, to Harvard!"

West had never been East before, and had never been on an airplane. His father went with him. West remembers that his father told him, "Corn, we're so proud you got here, but we know it will be hard, so all you need to stay is three Cs and a D."

"I appreciated that because I was pretty scared," he said.

Of course, he did far better at Harvard University than his father expected. At the end of the first semester, during which he took a graduate seminar in Hebrew along with his philosophy courses, he got three As and an A-. Eventually, West would graduate *magna cum laude* (Latin words that denote high academic distinction).

His father also advised his son to find out where the black people lived and get a haircut. He was wearing a full-blown Afro at the time. His father visited the predominantly black neighborhood of Roxbury—"where the black people lived."

"When he came back, he told me, 'It's going to be a struggle on the black side.'"

Cornel had found out where the black people lived, all right. But he didn't get that haircut. He studied philosophy at Harvard University, and took a heavy class load of 16 courses in his junior year, because he wanted to graduate in three years instead of the usual four. The reason was that he had to work to help pay his tuition and room and board.

He first worked two jobs, then three. He was on a dormitory crew, cleaning toilets. Eventually, he was promoted to washing dishes. And before he left Harvard University, he was able to work in the mailroom. Still, money was running out.

While at the university, West also performed volunteer work. He worked with the Black Panthers in their breakfast and prison outreach programs. He had gotten to know about the Panthers while still in California, and they were a big influence on him.

The Black Panthers had gained a bad reputation because they spoke in favor of revolution and violence and carried firearms. Yet, they also had some very good programs to help the needy.

"I would get up at six o'clock in the morning and go and feed the kids," West said. "We also talked to them about justice, freedom, equality, history. Then on Sundays, I would go to the Norfolk State Prison and talk to the prisoners. We had long dialogues with them."

A NARROW ESCAPE

In 1972, West was involved in a demonstration spearheaded by the university's Black Student Association. The

As a student at Harvard, West studied with enthusiasm, focusing on philosophy as well as Hebrew and Aramaic. He also began attending protests, serving as co-president of the Black Student Association, and working with the Black Panthers in their breakfast and prison outreach programs.

demonstration was organized to show support for the anti-government rebels in the African nation of Angola, and also to protest Harvard's investments in the oil industry. The group took over Massachusetts Hall, including the university president's office.

Even though Cornel was co-president of the Black Student Association, he was not inside the building. He was dealing at the time with some trumped-up charges of rape by the Cambridge Police. He and two black roommates,

Paul Nichols, of Boston, and Lenny Wallace, of Queens, New York, were arrested after the rape of a white female student who lived nearby.

The cops fingerprinted the "suspects" and took their mug shots. West said later that the police had encouraged the victim to identify him and his friends as the rapists, but she refused. All she knew, she said, was that a black man had committed the crime, but that the three arrested were not involved.

"Ironically," West said years later, "if it wasn't for this little white sister sitting there shaking, who said, 'No way, these are not the ones,' when the police were saying, 'C'mon, you know these are the guys. We've got them. We are resolving this case. C'mon now,' we'd have been just another statistic, another set of innocent brothers gone to Norfolk State Prison or somewhere for seven years."

Even if West had not been dealing with the police, he was too busy with school and personal activities to be tied up in a lengthy occupation of a university building.

"Here I am studying philosophy, taking Hebrew, studying Aramaic, working with the Black Panthers, working in the church, having the time of my life intellectually," he said. "Falling in love. A whole lot was going on."

Sylvester Monroe, a classmate of West's at Harvard University, recalled how he and West and other black students would sit up late into the night having rap sessions.

"We debated the necessity of taking all the university had to offer, but never losing ourselves to Harvard or any institution that would not accept us as the young, gifted beneficiaries of a post-Martin Luther King, Jr. black America, full of pride and possibility," Monroe wrote.

Among the black students who roomed together at Harvard's Leverett House dormitory, Monroe said, it was accepted that West was the best scholar, "though he never made us feel it."

"The important thing to keep in mind is that in 1970 I was coming out of a town, Sacramento, that was deeply affected by social movements," West said. "The civil rights movement, the Black Power movement, the Black Panther Party, had a major impact on me. Since, in a fundamental sense, I was convinced that I was, to the best of my ability, going to be myself within the Harvard context."

Monroe said West and the other black students adopted lyrics from "Thank You For Letting Me Be Myself Again," a song by the rock/funk group Sly and the Family Stone. It was sort of a "personal anthem," he said. Monroe explained that he and West were anxious to keep their ties to the black community back home.

"Part of it had to do with just acknowledging the richness of black culture, and, in some sense, trying to be persistent and downright courageous about just being myself," West said. "It was like, hey, you either accept me this way, or I just don't get accepted."

West says that one of his teachers, Martin Kilson, the first black tenured (permanent) professor at Harvard University, did not understand it. "He used to always say to me, 'Corn, intellectually you've got real potential, but if you don't shift culture, you ain't ever gonna make it in this context.'"

West said Kilson was upset that the black students were trying to identify themselves with "these street guys." But he told Kilson, who is now a good friend, "I'm learning, I'm changing. But the change is a combination of all these various forces that have shaped who I am."

Another resident of Leverett House was James Brown, later to become a host of Fox Sports Network. He said of

West, "He was always exploring the philosophical and constantly engaging in intellectual gymnastics. But as bright as the brother was, he was always a regular guy," Brown said. "He would always blend in. There was never any pretense, and never did he try to intimidate with his intellect. And yet, we all knew he was serious about his work. The brother maintained a beautiful balance."

After graduating from Harvard University at the age of 19, West was off to Princeton University on a fellowship—and he didn't have to clean toilets.

3

The Teacher

> "I think if I were to call myself anything it would be a man of letters who's deeply immersed in philosophical texts, in literary texts, deeply concerned also with scientific texts, but science much more as one element in the quest for wisdom rather than science as a way of gaining knowledge in order to dominate nature. So, in that sense, I have an intellectual curiosity that is quite broad, but I've never viewed myself as an academic or professional philosopher in a narrow sense."
> —Cornel West, *The Cornel West Reader*

Cornel West was nervous when he arrived at Princeton University. Princeton's philosophy department was the best in the country, and he was worried that the teachers—some of the greatest minds in philosophy—might undermine his Christian faith and challenge some of the other ideals he had developed at Harvard University. He need not have worried about the first concern.

"Nobody cared about religious faith," he wrote in *The Cornel West Reader.*

His two years as a graduate student at Princeton University were marked by hard work—he earned a master's degree in philosophy. Yet, they were calm compared to his days at Harvard University.

Among his favorite teachers was Richard Rorty. Listening to Rorty, he wrote, was "nearly as sweet as [the musical groups] the Dramatics, the Spinners, or the Main Ingredient, whom I then listened to daily for sanity."

It was during his two short years at Princeton University that he said he became convinced that the value and dignity of the individual was precious to him. He also felt that democracy, not just as a system of government, but as "a way of life and mode of being-in-the world," was equally important.

Democracy is a system of government in which the people run the government, rather than the government running the people. As Abraham Lincoln put it in his famous Gettysburg address during the Civil War, it is a government "of the people, by the people and for the people."

West's view is that American democracy does not always work out that way, especially for the poor and needy. In his book, *Race Matters,* he says the "major culprit" is the "ever-expanding market culture that puts everything and everyone up for sale."

What he wants is a system of government that takes care of the lowest members of the population along with the middle class and the rich.

West's earlier influences were Malcolm X and black nationalists, but he always knew their shortcomings. Of black nationalists, he said, "I worked with them on anti-racist issues—and we discussed, laughed and partied together weekly—but I always staked out my Christian version of democratic socialist values and politics." His major influence remained Dr. Martin Luther King, Jr., and the ideals of love and caring for all people.

After graduating from Princeton University, West returned to Harvard University under a Du Bois Fellowship to study philosophy for another two years. The fellowship was named after W.E.B. Du Bois, the black activist and scholar who lived from 1868 to 1963. Du Bois was one of the founders of the National Association for the Advancement of Colored People (NAACP), and was another man who struggled against odds to better the condition of black people.

After returning to Harvard University, West decided to try his hand at a novel. He developed a story about a black intellectual who wants to write, but recognizes that the black tradition is best expressed in music and oratory (public speaking). Unfortunately, the man goes deaf and can no longer hear the music that sustained him. Instead, he tries to recapture it in the written word.

Being unable to hear the music he loves, or listen to the great black preachers and others who exalt the spoken word, would have been tragic for West himself. So, he probably strongly identified with his character. The novel, however, was never published.

While at Harvard University, West married and had a son, Clifton, born in 1977, named after his brother. That marriage and two more ended in divorce. He has a daughter, Zeytun, born in 2000. He is reluctant to talk about his personal life.

As a black man in America, West has been subjected to major and minor racial insults. In an article in the *New York Times* in 1991, he told about an incident that occurred unexpectedly at Harvard University.

He was ready to teach a class on "Antigone," the story of a Greek mythological figure, when a student, who assumed this black man was the janitor, asked him to get more chairs.

"I brought the chairs in," he said, "and when the rest of the class got there, I stood up and started to lecture on Antigone's famous love song about humans being so noble on the one hand and so cruel on the other."

After Harvard University, West took his first full-time teaching job. It was at Union Theological Seminary in New York City. It was 1977 and he was 24. He was greatly honored to inherit the office of Reinhold Niebuhr, a famous philosopher and theologian who taught at Union from 1928 to 1960. Many of Niebuhr's ideas and activities influenced West.

Niebuhr was an evangelical minister who had a deep concern for the common man. This concern led to one of his most famous battles. It was against Henry Ford and the Ford Motor Company while Niebuhr was pastor of the Bethel Evangelical Church in Detroit. Most of the country was praising Henry Ford for introducing the assembly line, and paying his workers the then-unheard-of wage of $5 a day, but Niebuhr attacked the very idea of industrialization.

"I cut my eyeteeth fighting Ford," he once said.

He focused on the injustices that followed in the wake of industrialization. He preached about poor housing, the lack of job security or insurance, lack of retirement benefits, not to mention the workers' exhaustion from the grueling life on the assembly line.

He became a friend of Walter Reuther, a fiery labor leader and head of the United Auto Workers Union. He also joined the Socialist Party. (Socialists favor government ownership of the means of production.) Although Niebuhr modified his views later in life, he remained a severe critic of the capitalist system, as has Cornel West.

Niebuhr had no patience with phonies, and scorned people with the self-righteous belief that they had a corner on the truth. These were the same feelings Cornel West often expressed. Niebuhr was also famous as the author of the "Serenity Prayer:"

"Oh, God, give us serenity to accept what cannot be changed, courage to change what should be changed, and wisdom to distinguish the one from the other."

In a slightly modified form it became the slogan of Alcoholics Anonymous and other self-help organizations.

Niebuhr was a very popular teacher at Union, and his door was always open to students. He died in 1971. Another famed teacher at Union was Paul Tillich, a German-born theologian and philosopher, who fled his homeland when the Nazis took over. Niebuhr had invited him to Union.

West felt honored to follow in the footsteps of such great educators and Christian thinkers.

"Union was the greatest Christian seminary in the country," he said in an interview. "Niebhur was there when I was a freshman at Harvard. My teachers had me read Niebuhr at that time and I said, 'This is my soul mate.' And then they gave me his office!"

West referred to his seven years at Union as a "magnificent time." He joined the Democratic Socialists of America—"with my dear friend Michael Harrington."

Harrington was a man who devoted his life to raising awareness of the fact that poverty continued to exist in America, despite the general prosperity of the nation. Hundreds of thousands of people were being left behind. His most famous book, *The Other America: Poverty in the*

United States (1962), helped convince President John F. Kennedy to ask Congress for federal action to reduce poverty.

TO PARIS AND BACK

After Kennedy's assassination in 1963, President Lyndon B. Johnson began a series of anti-poverty measures called the "War on Poverty." Harrington became an adviser to Johnson on the "war." Among results of their efforts were the Economic Opportunity Act of 1964, the Appalachian Redevelopment Act of 1965, and the Medicare Act that same year.

Harrington continued to write, speak, and lecture on poverty for the rest of his life. He died in 1989. West got to know Harrington in 1982 while he was teaching at Union Theological Seminary.

"We traveled the country together," he said, "to keep track of inequality."

Among the matters that concerned them were police brutality, dilapidated housing, and healthcare. They wanted to help the poor and needy.

"Harrington was a charismatic figure," West said. "We wanted to make sure that democracy was robust in America, that working people and poor people had access to a job with a living wage."

One problem he had with the Democratic Socialists was that most of the members were determinedly secular—concerned with worldly affairs rather than spiritual ones. Such people looked at him askance because of his religious views.

"They would say, 'He's religious. When is he going to grow up?'" West said.

At that time, West was speaking regularly at black churches during Sunday morning services. "They asked me to, as a lay Christian."

West does not like to be labeled with any particular religious denomination, although he was raised a Baptist. "I'm ecumenical," he said, meaning he has no church affiliation, but embraces the whole religious ethos.

"There is such a thing as secular arrogance," he said. "But there is also Christian arrogance. It can be just as vicious."

West earned his doctorate in philosophy from Princeton University while teaching at Union. He then moved to Yale University, in New Haven, Connecticut. But trouble awaited him there.

"I made history at Yale," he said. "I was the first Yale professor arrested on Yale property."

It was 1987, and he was involved in a demonstration on behalf of clerical workers who were trying to form a union.

"They were making $11,000 a year," he said. "The university was paying them nothing. You know, New Haven is one of the poorest cities in the country."

He and other demonstrators were charged with desecration of property. West insisted on being arrested on the Yale University campus, which embarrassed the administration.

"They kept us in jail for eight or nine hours," he said.

At that time, West was the American correspondent for the Paris publication, *Le Monde Diplomatique*. He wrote articles about American issues, including race relations. His writing attracted attention in the French capital and he received an invitation to teach at the University of Paris.

His idea was to take a sabbatical (leave of absence) so he could teach in Paris for a semester. But Yale University officials, angered by his arrest, refused to grant him the leave time.

"So I decided to teach in both places," he said.

He flew to Paris every week, teaching courses in philosophy and American race relations every Thursday and Friday. Then he would fly back in time to teach his regular classes at Yale University on Monday morning.

"It was too much for me," he said. "I decided to leave Yale, and go back to Union. I thought I would be there the rest of my life."

Then he got a call from Toni Morrison, a famous author of African descent. Her major novels include *The Bluest Eye, Song of Solomon, Sula, Tar Baby, Beloved*, and *Jazz*. Morrison won the Pulitzer Prize in 1987 and the Nobel Prize for Literature in 1993, the highest honor a writer can attain.

Morrison is also a highly regarded teacher. She taught at Yale University, Bard College, Rutgers University, and Princeton University, where she became the Robert F. Goheen Professor of the Council of the Humanities in 1989. She also has lectured at Harvard University and Trinity College, Cambridge, in England. She managed to catch Cornel West after a year back at Union.

"She said, 'Cornel, we have a chance to create an intellectual neighborhood,'" he said. "God, I loved that idea. So I went there in 1988—and that's what we did."

He was director of the African-American studies program at Princeton University for six years. Morrison had high praise for his work there.

"Cornel shows us how the academy *ought* to work," she said. "He used his powerful intellect as a harvester, not a weapon. Instead of carving out a small place for himself, he makes this place bigger."

"It was magnificent," West said, using one of his favorite words. "So many different people were hired. It became one of the great centers of African-American studies, if not *the* greatest."

But Harvard University began calling to him again. A man named Henry Louis Gates, Jr. wanted to establish an even greater African-American studies program at Harvard, and he was trying to hire black scholars to run it.

GATES' DREAM TEAM

Gates, who was born in 1950, was a young black man in a hurry, just like Cornel West. He took over Harvard's African-American Studies Department in 1991, when he was only 41, determined to make it work.

One of the problems he faced was the feeling among some academics that an African-American study program was not a legitimate curriculum for a major university. He was determined to prove them wrong.

Gates, known to his friends as "Skip," was born in Keyser, West Virginia. Like West, he had a family that encouraged him to excel at everything he did in life. He attended Potomac State College of West Virginia University, and then entered Yale University. He was one of only 95 other black students accepted there in 1973.

He graduated *summa cum laude* (Latin words that denote the highest academic distinction) from Yale University in 1973, and won a fellowship to study in England at Clare College, Cambridge University. He then returned to the United States, and after a variety of jobs, went back to Yale to complete work on his doctorate. In 1979, he joined the Yale faculty as an assistant professor of English.

Gates was upset when Yale University passed him over for tenure. He left and went to Cornell University, where he was named the W.E.B. Du Bois Professor of

Literature. He was the first African-American man to hold such a position at Cornell.

In 1990, Gates took a professorship at Duke University in Durham, North Carolina. By that time, he had married a white woman. Interracial couples were not readily accepted in the South at that time. [It also didn't sit well with the Duke administration when he testified at a First Amendment (free speech) case in Florida involving the hip-hop band 2 Live Crew, which was charged with using obscene lyrics.]

Although his participation in the case was minimal, he was criticized by fellow professors, Duke officials, and even the student newspaper. Gates decided it was time to head back North.

He accepted an offer at Harvard University to head up its failing African-American studies program. His titles were W.E.B. Du Bois Professor of the Humanities, Chair of the Afro-American Studies Department, and Director of the W.E.B. Du Bois Institute for Afro-American Studies.

"What we're trying to do at Harvard is to create, well, quite frankly, what I hope will be the greatest center of intellection concerning persons of African descent in the Old World and the New World," he said at the time.

What he set out to do was create a "dream team" of black scholars and teachers. And the name of Cornel West was high on his list. Writing in the *Boston Globe* in May, 1991, about Gates, John Powers noted: "Around the Yard (the Harvard campus) the man is being hyped as some sort of black Messiah."

"The arrival of Gates, the most notable scholar of African-American studies in the land," Powers wrote, "has provoked uncommon curiosity and speculation around Cambridge.

"Can he revive the university's stagnant African-American program? Can he recruit other black professors to the school's white-bread faculty of arts and sciences? And can Harvard hang on to him?"

Peter Gomes, then professor of Christian morals at Harvard University, said of Gates, "He's the Second Coming. Or maybe he's the First Coming. He makes all the difference in the world."

"We are placing all the burdens on him that we would place on Moses," added Gomes, who doubled as acting director of the W.E.B. Du Bois Institute for African-American Research.

Gates asked, "Where else could I go in America and build an African-American program from scratch? The challenge of reversing two decades of failure, that's exciting," he added. "It's like a dare."

Indeed, it was kind of "a dare" that Gates put to Cornel West and the other black scholars he was determined to recruit to Harvard University. The African-American studies program at Harvard began in 1969 when student protests, including the occupation of University Hall, arrests, and a student strike, convinced officials to begin such a curriculum.

At first, Cornel West wasn't interested in Harvard University. He was among a number of black academics invited by Gates to join his department, and was one of many who refused. The prospect of joining a faculty that had only two other black full professors was clearly off-putting. "There was a fear of scholarly loneliness, of stepping into a void," Gomes said. "With all the good will, there were no colleagues."

But Gates wouldn't take no for an answer, and he eventually got his "dream team." In addition to Cornel West, it consisted of K. Anthony Appiah, who is the first African American to earn a doctorate from Cambridge University in England, and William Julius Wilson, a scholar and writer, whose 1987 book, *The Truly Disadvantaged*, described the terrible effects of job loss on the urban ghetto.

"Getting to know Cornel West has been one of the genuine pleasures of my life," Gates said. "I have never met a person who combines genuine passion for the plight of human beings less fortunate than he with intellectual insight and the capacity on his feet to communicate both that depth of compassion and to propose solutions that would cure the suffering that he is describing."

Unfortunately, after nine years of a very satisfying experience for West at Harvard University, it all went sour.

4

Harvard
Dust-Up

"Afro-American studies was never meant to be solely for
Afro-Americans. It was meant to try to redefine what it
means to be human, what it means to be modern, what it
means to be American, because people of African descent
in this country are profoundly human, profoundly modern,
profoundly American. And so to the degree to which they
can see the riches that we have to offer as well as see our
shortcomings, is the degree to which they can more fully
understand the modern and what modernity is all about,
and more fully understand the American experience."
—Cornel West, *The Cornel West Reader*

Cornel West was ready to leave Princeton University. For
one thing, he didn't like administrative work. He was
director of the African-American studies program and
paperwork was a grind for him. Besides, after six years, his
restless spirit needed a change.

Dr. Henry Louis Gates, Jr. (left) was very interested in adding Cornel West to his faculty at Harvard's Afro-American Studies Department. Although West at first showed little interest in joining the nearly all-white Harvard faculty, Gates persuaded him to make the leap. West's relationship with Harvard lasted nine years.

Gates promised Cornel he wouldn't have to do any administrative work at Harvard. Gates also told him he would be the core of the "dream team." Gates likened hiring Appiah to "acquiring a power forward on a basketball team." But he needed a brilliant guard, and that would be West.

"It would be unprecedented for a black person to leave a kingdom—and he had a kingdom as director of the

Afro-American studies program at Princeton—and become part of a team," Gates said. But that didn't seem to bother West.

Gates added that he never would have gotten William Julius Wilson from the University of Chicago if Cornel hadn't come first. Gates also recruited Evelyn Brooks Higginbotham from the University of Pennsylvania. Her husband, A. Leon Higginbotham, Jr., noted jurist and civil rights leader from Philadelphia, was retiring from the United States Third Circuit Court of Appeals.

"He [West] is our black Jeremiah," Gates, referring to the biblical prophet who preached 600 years before the birth of Jesus. Jeremiah was known for speaking truths that many people did not want to hear—he didn't care for phonies either.

"He is the only person on the intellectual scene capable of inheriting the mantle of Reinhold Niebuhr," said Ronald Theimann, dean of the Harvard Divinity School. "And if he does, he will weave into that mantle so many new and different threads it may no longer be recognizable as the same cloth."

West must have enjoyed hearing himself compared to one of his heroes, Reinhold Niebuhr, whose office he had inherited at Union Theological Seminary.

West was married to Elleni Gebre Amlak, an Ethiopian, at the time. They had a home in Addis Ababa, Ethiopia, where they spent their summers. Everything went along fine at Harvard University for a long time. Its African-American program was hailed around the country as leading the way in that field with its brilliant array of scholars and teachers.

Then, on July 1, 2001, Lawrence H. Summers, an econ-omist who had been U.S. Treasury Secretary in the Clinton

Administration, was named the 27th president of Harvard University. Summers replaced Neil L. Rudenstein, the man who had brought Henry Louis Gates, Jr. to Harvard to repair the university's lagging African-American studies program.

TROUBLE WITH THE NEW PRESIDENT

Summers, who was 47 years old at the time, was thoroughly familiar with Harvard University. He had been a professor of political economy and public finance there, and received his Ph.D. from Harvard in 1982. He also had taught economics at the Massachusetts Institute of Technology.

In 1993, he went to Washington as an undersecretary of the Treasury Department for international affairs. Then, as deputy secretary, he worked with the Treasury Secretary Robert E. Rubin (also a Harvard University graduate) and Alan Greenspan, chairman of the Federal Reserve System. On July 22, 1999, Summers was confirmed by the Senate as Treasury Secretary. Among Summers' many achievements as Treasury Secretary, was helping engineer a reduction of the national debt, extending the life of Social Security and Medicare trust finds, and leading the deregulation effort that relieved many businesses of the burden of federal rules and regulations that interfered with their operations. After leaving the Treasury Department in January 2001, he taught for a time at the Brookings Institution in Washington.

Summers had the kind of qualifications for which Harvard University was looking. He was invited to apply for the presidency. That he had no background to speak of in African-American studies, and apparently had spent little time examining the issue of race in America, was not considered.

One of Summers' first actions was to call a meeting with Cornel West. West thought it would be a cordial meeting. After all, they were both cancer survivors. But it did not go well.

"I never saw Summers before," he said. "He just tears into me like I do not know. He accuses me of missing classes three weeks in a row to work for Bill Bradley." (Bill Bradley is a former United States Senator from New Jersey.)

"He obviously hadn't done his homework. The only day I missed was when I went to Ethiopia for an AIDS conference—one day in eight years. I looked him straight in the eye and said, 'What kind of person do you think I am?'"

West said when he worked for Bradley, he would fly out to the campaign on Thursdays and fly back for classes on Mondays. "They thought I was crazy," he said of the campaign aides.

But Summers had other complaints. He told West that he hadn't written anything for a long time, that he should be ashamed of himself for "associating with hip-hop" by making a rap CD, and supporting candidates nobody had any respect for.

The reference was not to Bradley, who was a highly thought of former basketball star of the New York Knicks, and who had a distinguished Senate career behind him, nor Ralph Nader, on whose presidential campaign West also worked. The reference was to the Reverend Al Sharpton.

West had high regard for Sharpton and was helping Sharpton plan his presidential campaign. But Sharpton was a controversial figure in New York. (More about Sharpton later.) Summers told West it was time he wrote a book on philosophy. That took West by surprise because he had written extensively about philosophy, and had written a total of 16 books, not to mention dozens of articles for popular and academic publications. West said he suspected that Summers came from "a particular group of people who had been targeting me for some time."

"He was making pronouncements about my work that he never read, pronouncements about my CD that he never heard—and he had never met me before," West said.

Summers also accused West of grade inflation. That was a subject of considerable interest and debate on college campuses, especially in African-American studies. Professors were accused of awarding grades that the students hadn't really earned. But West challenged Summers to compare his grades with those of other teachers and he would find no evidence of grade inflation.

"I told him I was as concerned about that as he was," West said.

He said Summers asked him what his approach to West would have been if West were in his shoes.

"I'll tell you exactly," he said he told Summers. "I would say, 'It's very nice to meet you, professor, and I know we both have a high commitment to excellence, to be sure the students get the best education. How can we work together?'"

"We assume we have some common enterprise. He doesn't know the first thing about leadership. The president of Harvard University has to be told *that*?"

WEST RETURNS TO PRINCETON

The meeting, which was private, of course, occurred in October 2001. But by December, word had gotten to the press. The *New York Times* carried the controversy on page one. Any dust-up at America's most prestigious university was news.

During his years at Harvard, West remained committed both to teaching and to political activism, working on the presidential campaigns of Bill Bradley, Ralph Nader, and Reverend Al Sharpton. West's experience at Harvard would change, however, when Harvard chose Lawrence Summers—former U.S. Treasury Secretary—to be its president. Summers disapproved of West's activism and his approach to teaching. After a number of personality clashes with Summers, West resigned his position at Harvard.

"He got real nervous," West said of Summers. "He got calls from the trustees."

Summers wanted another meeting with West. This time everything was different. "We had a wonderful talk," said West, who is the forgiving type anyway. "He said he really wanted to apologize. He said, 'You were absolutely right, I had no right to say those things.' We shook hands."

Then things got sticky.

"I read in the *New York Times* the next day that he had refused to apologize to me. I called him and asked him if he had apologized, and he said of course he had. He blamed the *Times* for getting the story wrong."

But there were other issues. Summers told West he wanted to monitor West's progress on his next scholarly work by getting a progress report every two or three months.

"Professors do not have supervisors, brother," West told a reporter. "Professors are free agents to do their work, because there is a trust in their judgment about how they go about doing that work. Criticism is fine," West said. "Trashing based on no evidence is irresponsible."

West also was annoyed that Summers had not expressed any get-well sentiments when he had serious prostate cancer surgery. Most other colleagues and friends had done so. A card from Summers did finally arrive—two months after the surgery, he said.

"He struck me very much as a bull in a china shop, and as a bully, in a very delicate and dangerous situation," West said of Summers.

Summers has had very little to say about the affair publicly. He generally refused to comment on it, except to say he regretted that it happened. He made later efforts to reach out to West, both by phone and in writing, but West was tired of the feud. He decided to go back to Princeton University. His colleague, K. Anthony Appiah, had already left for Princeton.

Princeton University also wanted to get Henry Louis Gates, Jr. and William Julius Wilson to defect. Gates had been seriously considering transferring to Princeton. He had even visited the area with a real estate agent, looking for possible homes. But Gates announced in December 2002 that he would remain at Harvard University. He said Summers had appealed to him, even visiting him at his home on Martha's Vineyard in Massachusetts.

At a party at Summers' home in Cambridge celebrating the start of a new school year, Summers told the guests, including Gates, that he expected to see them all at a similar party the next year. Gates said later that Summers' visit to Martha's Vineyard and his remarks at the party convinced him to stay at Harvard University.

"I came away convinced that Afro-American studies would occupy a central role in President Summers' vision of Harvard in the 21st century," Gates told the *New York Times*.

Summers himself told the newspaper that the "study of the Afro-American experience is an essential area at Harvard," and added that Gates had "contributed to Harvard enormously."

"His leadership, along with that of his colleagues here, and the scholars we will recruit in coming months and years, will maintain and extend Harvard's leadership in this vital area," Summers said.

"Many of the students came here to study with Anthony and Cornel," Gates said about Harvard, "and even with me. It was important that someone provide continuity, and I decided that someone should be me."

Still, West was not the only Harvard University professor Summers had upset. In one meeting, he asked the head of the School of Education to justify the very existence of his program. He told a law professor that a question she asked him was "stupid."

West was welcomed like a conquering hero when he returned to Princeton University. He became the Class of 1943 University Professor of Religion. Among those who welcomed him was Princeton President Shirley M. Tilghman.

"Cornel West, who is known for his intellectual contributions in the study of religion and for challenging those both inside and outside of academia to think about critical issues of race, was a popular and dedicated teacher during his previous tenure at Princeton, and we are pleased that he has decided to return," she said.

"It would be accurate to say that he has reshaped religious studies in such a way that his area of interest is now seen as central to the field," said Jeffrey Stout, a professor of religion at Princeton University.

"The Department of Religion is delighted to welcome back Cornel West," said Professor Martha Himmelfarb, chairwoman of the department. "During his years here he brought extraordinary energy to his undergraduate teaching, and he helped to attract and train an exceptional group of graduate students."

For his part, West said, "I am excited to return to the greatest center for humanistic studies in the country. I look forward to being a part of President Tilghman's vision that promotes high quality intellectual conversation mediated with respect."

What he meant was, he was happy to be in a place where he could have some intelligent conversations with people who respected him and his views. West did seem to have found a home in his cozy, book-lined office in the fortress-like 1879 Hall at Princeton University, with his favorite restaurant, the Annex, within walking distance. He could have his veal parmesan, and banter with colleagues and students, to his heart's content.

One gets the impression that he much prefers being outside the walls of that monster of a building, and getting back to the people. He calls himself a "public teacher," which means he is in the public eye more than he is hidden away among his books.

West does not e-mail his messages—he doesn't even own a computer. He doesn't have a cell phone. He writes in longhand. He calls himself "old school." It's also why he wears those dark, three-piece suits. They bring back memories of the black preachers and jazz musicians of his youth, men of dignity and humility. About the Afro hairdo he continues to wear, he said, "I don't have time to get a haircut."

He is a classical violinist, an instrument he began studying as a child. He likes to relax with a pipe. He remains concerned about the cancer that was surgically removed from his prostate in November 2002. It was an especially aggressive form of cancer, and he still thinks about the possibility of it recurring and spreading through his body.

But he is trim and healthy looking, and full of the old energy that keeps him going around the country to spread his philosophy of love, and to protest against inequality. He does all this while handling a full load of classes and lectures at Princeton University.

For instance, in 2002, he traveled to Minneapolis, Minnesota, at the invitation of the entertainer Prince for the singer's "Xenophobia" conference. Then it was off to

Washington, D.C. for a protest on Middle East Policy, where he ended up being arrested. It was then off to Sydney, Australia, for the filming of his role in the sequel to the film, *The Matrix, The Matrix Reloaded.*

Indeed, Cornel West shows no sign of cutting back on his schedule.

5

Inspiring
the Young

> "The basic aim of a democratic regime is to curb the use of arbitrary powers—especially of government and economic institutions—against its citizens. Based on this uncontroversial criterion, the history of American democracy in regard to black people from 1776 to 1965 was a colossal failure. This also holds for red, brown, and yellow peoples. For one generation —35 years— we have embarked on a multiracial democracy with significant breakthroughs and glaring silences."
>
> —Cornel West, *Race Matters*

One day in September 1993, Cornel West and his wife, Elleni, were making a trip from Princeton to New York City. West had an appointment in Harlem with photographers to take his picture for the cover of his book, *Race Matters*.

He was feeling quite content. He had delivered a morning lecture on Plato's *Republic* for his European Cultural Studies course, and an afternoon lecture on W.E.B. Du Bois' *The Souls of Black Folk* for his Afro-American Cultural Studies course.

He thought both lectures had gone well. As he drove into the Lincoln Tunnel, he was thinking of something Du Bois wrote: "The problem of the 20th century is the problem of the color line." As recounted in *Race Matters*, he was thinking of his own goal in life—"To speak the truth to power with love so that the quality of everyday life for ordinary people is enhanced and white supremacy stripped of its authority and legitimacy."

A mouthful to be sure. Yet, his meaning, expressed many times in his books and lectures, is clear. West wants to confront America's leaders about the race issue, but he wants to do it with love. He wants the life of ordinary people improved and white dominance deprived of its power to hurt. A tall order, but those have been the guiding principles of his life.

West was entertaining these thoughts as he arrived in Manhattan. He was surprised to find that the traffic was not as bad as usual. A good omen. It was going to be a lucky day! It was going to be even better if he and Elleni had time to stop at their favorite restaurant, Sweetwater's, for soul food. That would depend on how things went with the photo shoot.

He dropped Elleni off for an appointment in the uptown section of Manhattan. He parked his Cadillac in a nearby lot and headed for the corner to catch a taxi to East Harlem, where the photo shoot was to take place on the roof of an apartment building. The photographers wanted to shoot him with the city skyline in the background. He waited patiently for taxis. One after another, the cabs slowed long enough for the driver to take a good look at the bearded black man trying to flag them, and then sped away. Nine cabs repeated the procedure.

"A wonderful white sister, about 55 or so, walks up," he said. "In about two minutes, a cab stopped for her. She turned to me and said, 'This is ridiculous. You've been standing out here all this time and I just get a taxi right away.'"

As the woman hopped in the cab and it drove away, West thought about other times he had suffered such insults, and he remembered even worse racist attacks on other people in recent history. "Yet the memories cut like a merciless knife at my soul as I waited on that godforsaken corner," he wrote.

West finally decided to take a subway, which meant he had to walk three long blocks to reach the site of the photo shoot.

"I had to catch my moral breath as I approached the white photographer and white female cover designer," he wrote.

He didn't want to take his anger out on these people, even though their white skins reminded him of the insult.

"I decided not to dwell on this everyday experience of black New Yorkers," he wrote. "And we had a good time talking, posing, and taking pictures."

"The anger has to be processed and digested," he said, "so you don't end up hating others, increasing the bigotry in the world."

When he picked up his wife later, he told her about his experience and they spoke, again, of their frequent fantasy of moving to Addis Ababa, Ethiopia, her native land. It was tempting to just go away—forever. But West knew that wasn't his destiny.

They went to Sweetwater's, "and the ugly memories faded in the face of soulful music, soulful food, and soulful folk."

"As we rode back to Princeton, above the soothing black music of Van Harper's "Quiet Storm" on the radio, we talked about what race matters have meant to the American past and how much race matters in the American present."

"And I vowed to be more vigilant and virtuous in my efforts to meet the formidable challenges of Plato and Du Bois. For me, it is an urgent question of power and morality, for others, it is an everyday matter of life and death."

Plato, a Greek philosopher who lived about 300 years before the birth of Jesus, wrote a series of works based on dialogues, or conversations, with the great Greek thinker Socrates. Together they explored the meaning of life, what it means to be human, and what the ideal government would be.

THE RACIAL PROFILE

Despite living in the rarefied atmosphere of academia, West has had to deal with the everyday problems of being a black man in a predominantly white nation with a long history of keeping blacks powerless.

Once, on his way to a teaching job at Williams College, in Williamstown, Massachusetts, in the 1980s, he was pulled over by a state trooper on false charges of trafficking cocaine.

West was wearing his usual three-piece suit, there were books and papers in the car, but the police officer didn't see any of that. He saw a black man. West tried to explain that he was a philosophy professor on his way to teach at a college.

"Yeah, and I'm the Flying Nun," the trooper sneered. "Come on, nigger."

"I was stopped three times in my first ten days in Princeton for driving too slowly on a residential street with a speed limit of twenty-five miles per hour," he wrote.

Reverend Al Sharpton is credited with raising the issue of "racial profiling" by police, and since then it has become a national cause. Police departments all over the country have become sensitive to the issue. In Philadelphia, former Police Commissioner John Timoney required officers to report, in detail why they had made a traffic stop to avoid accusations that the driver and the occupants of the car had been targeted because of their race or ethnicity. Other departments around the country followed suit.

Even West's son, Clifton, has run into discrimination. In fact, *Race Matters* is dedicated to him: "To my wonderful son, Clifton Louis West, who combats daily the hidden injuries of race with the most potent of weapons—love of self and others."

THE PROBLEM PEOPLE

West notes that both liberals and conservatives often view blacks as problems. Many liberals, he points out, think government programs will solve the problem, like in the days of former President Lyndon Johnson's Great Society. Many conservatives, on the other hand, think that blacks—especially young black men in urban ghettoes—must change their ways. They should stay married, support their children, and obey the law.

Both approaches wind up at the same conclusion: blacks are a problem people. He quotes W.E.B. Du Bois responding to what he called the "unasked question" in his book, *The Souls of Black Folk* (1903):

> They approach me in a half-hesitant sort of way, eye me curiously or compassionately, and then instead of saying directly, How does it feel to be a problem?

They say, I know an excellent colored man in my town. ... Do not these Southern outrages make your blood boil? At these I smile, or am interested, or reduce the boiling to a simmer, as the occasion may require. To the real question, How does it feel to be a problem? I answer seldom a word.

In *Race Matters*, West writes "Nearly a century later, we confine discussions about race in America to the 'problems' black people pose for whites, rather than consider what this way of viewing black people reveals about us as a nation."

The burden is on black people to shape up, he says. "The implication is that only certain Americans can define what it means to be American—and the rest must simply 'fit in.' The emergence of strong black-nationalist sentiments among blacks, especially among young people, is a revolt against this sense of having to 'fit in.'"

West speaks frequently to young people. "I tell them there's always the possibility of self-discipline, and being determined, and being compassionate," he said in an interview.

"There's such a thing as individual responsibility, no matter how bad the circumstances are. But you also tell them that there are many of us fighting to change their circumstances so it would be easier. Whatever skills they have, whether it be athletic, scientific, intellectual, they need to accent it, cultivate it, develop it against the grain. Then you remind them that they come out of a history of people who have been fighting against the grain. Their forefathers who were slaves, who were Jim Crowed, who were discriminated against, they were fighting against the grain, too. So they're not the first ones to fight against the grain, even though it's very difficult."

"Then, most importantly, you tell them that you care for them, that they are not forgotten. That's the one thing I like about Sharpton," he said. "You want to hit on a national level a message to young folk that they're cared for, that there are people who are speaking to power, speaking on a national level, concerned about your plight, your predicament, because for so long their suffering has been invisible."

He said the young "want people to believe in them, and they want people who are highly visible to do so, so they can really believe in themselves. But you have to fight battles, political battles, to help change their conditions and circumstances."

"Part of the problem these days is that too many young people of all colors are not loved enough," he said. "They're not focused on enough, they don't receive enough attention—the opposite of what I had growing up.

"It's hard to believe you're worthy if you haven't been loved early on, let alone return it. It's tough for all human beings, but especially for people in bad social and economic circumstances."

He speaks frequently to prisoners. "I tell them they would be surprised at the number of persons who appear to be free outside the walls, but are very much in prison in their hearts and minds and souls. Freedom is actually the kind of thing that can be worked on and worked on wherever you are. You want to make sure you do the time rather than the time doing you."

He tells them to "take advantage of the time, read, write, try to have conversations that are meaningful. You can change and transform in prison."

"I talk about the great folk who came out of prisons— Jesus, Martin Luther King, Jr., Gandhi, Malcolm X. Prison

West remains committed to expressing his political views through peaceful protest. Here he sits with other protesters arrested in Washington, D.C., during a demonstration against Israel's incursion into the West Bank.

has historically been a place where you linger and come out the same or worse than when you went in."

He might have added the name of Cornel West to that list of former prisoners. In April 2002, West was still recovering from cancer surgery when he decided to join Rabbi Michael Lerner in a demonstration at the State Department in Washington over the Israeli-Palestinian conflict.

His doctors had warned him not to participate in any demonstrations in which there was a chance of being roughed up. But he didn't listen to them. He and Rabbi Lerner made a strange pair on the sidewalk as they spoke into microphones about the Middle East's most difficult problem. Lerner is a large, rather rumpled man with unkempt hair, while West is dapper, as always, in his three-piece suit and trim beard and Afro. But they both had the same message.

"We talked about the suffering on both sides, both the Israelis and Palestinians," West said in an interview. "It's just been so overwhelming, and it has to do with the mediocre and myopic [near-sighted] leadership of both [Ariel] Sharon and [Yasir] Arafat."

They were also critical of United States Mid-East policies that they felt tended to put more value on the lives of Israelis than those of Palestinians.

"We're just as upset that Palestinians are being killed as Israelis," he said. "That view is not popular in America."

It wasn't the first time the two men had lectured together on the subject of Israel and Palestine, but this time they decided on an act of civil disobedience to call attention to their views. They sat in the middle of C Street outside the State Department and refused to move.

West winced as the cops came and dragged him and other demonstrators away bodily. He thought about those fresh stitches.

Then, apparently to teach the protestors a lesson, the cops kept them in the Washington lockup for 13 hours, without food. They wound up with a $100 fine—but luckily West's stitches held.

INTO THE FUNK

West once described America as a "hotel civilization"—"obsessed with comfort and convenience and contentment."

As a speaker, West believes he may sometimes get himself into trouble by being too truthful. Here we see him, in his customary three-piece suit, Afro, and goatee, animatedly addressing an audience.

A hotel is "a fusion of the home and the market (that) makes you feel at home if you have the cash to pay."

When you leave the room it's dirty, but when you come back it's clean. He said in a hotel you are shielded from the unpleasantness of the world outside the hotel.

He likes to use the word "funk." He defines it as the "underside, the hidden side, of America, the side we would rather conceal, but we know it's always there.

"The funk of America would be slavery, Jim Crow, what happened to the Indians. We want to hide it as if it didn't exist. Look at the prisons, look at what's happening to working people these days. We hide it. Newspapers don't even have a labor page anymore; they have a business page. What happened to all these working people?"

"Well, once in a while we'll do a story here and there, but we push that aside, all these realities. We do that in our own lives as well, suppress it, and think somehow the return of the suppressed won't happen. But it does."

West believes that his plainspoken way of expressing the truth as he sees it sometimes gets him into trouble. He used the example of the ancient Greek philosopher Socrates, who questioned authority and was eventually sentenced to death.

"That's what gets people in trouble, all the way back to Socrates. Socrates said, 'The plain speaking of mine is the cause of my unpopularity. I infect them with the perplexity I feel myself.'"

West said, "It's speaking the truth as you understand it that unsettles people, deeply unsettles people. Jesus is the best example of it. The wonderful thing about Jesus and Socrates is that they were sharing their own sense of struggle. Not as if they bring some smooth truth and upset others; they're upset, too.

"Jesus said what he was doing was something he'd rather not do. Malcolm X would get up there and talk about white supremacy, but he knew white supremacy was in him, not just in other people. He was struggling himself; he had been a pimp, he had been out there following the same kind of orientation.

"Martin [Luther King, Jr.] was out there talking about sin and evil, fighting and struggling, but he was undergoing those things himself.

"We're all in the muck and the mud together. We're all in the funk together."

That's one of the reasons West loves blues music so much. It describes the funk, but it also shows the way out of it.

"Socrates didn't have as much compassion as he should have," West continued. "He was arrogant. He never cries. He never sheds one tear. Jesus wept. That's a big difference. People who never cry never love deeply.

"Socrates lived too much in the mind. Questioning is very important, but you have to wed the spirituality of questioning with the spirituality of loving, and if they don't go hand in hand, you're missing something."

6

The Missing Heroes

> "The temptation of despair is predicated on a world with no room for black space, place, or face. It feeds on a black futurelessness and black hopelessness— a situation in which visions and dreams of possibility have dried up like raisins in the sun. This nihilism leads to lives of drift, lives in which any pleasure, especially instant gratification, is the primary means of feeling alive."
>
> —Cornel West, *The Cornel West Reader*

Cornel West has expressed deep concern about the quality of black leadership in America today. There are exceptions, of course, but in *Race Matters*, he said, "There has not been a time in the history of black people in this country when the quantity of politicians and intellectuals was so great, yet the quality of both groups has been so low."

"Just when one would have guessed that black America was flexing its political and intellectual muscles, *rigor mortis* seems to have set in."

The problem, as he sees it, is the character of the black middle class, from which leaders often come. He feels that today's black middle class is too self-centered, too complacent, too unconcerned about the underclass to be very effective.

"For the most part," he wrote, "the dominant outlooks and lifestyles of today's black middle class discourage the development of high quality political and intellectual leaders."

Pointing to the black heroes of the past—Frederick Douglass, W.E.B. Du Bois, Marcus Garvey, Malcolm X, Martin Luther King, Jr., Ida B. Wells, and Fannie Lou Hamer—West wonders where today's heroes are, which brings up the subject of the Reverend Al Sharpton.

Born in 1954 in Brooklyn, New York, Sharpton had made unsuccessful runs for the United States Senate and mayor of New York City. When he decided to run for the Democratic nomination for president in the 2004 election, Cornel West headed his exploratory committee. West had also supported Sharpton in his bids for Senate and mayor.

"I met him in the 1980s," West said in an interview. "He was the first to call attention to police brutality and racial profiling. He was much more of a black nationalist in his early days. He's much different today."

That difference owes a lot to Cornel West. In 1988, Sharpton and West held a historic meeting at Sylvia's restaurant in Harlem.

"I just confronted him with a question," West said. "I asked, 'Do you come out of the house of Martin Luther King, Jr. or do you come out of the house of Elijah

Muhammad? (Late leader of the Black Muslims and a black nationalist.) The choice is yours."

West said he told Sharpton, "I come out of the legacy of Martin Luther King, Jr." He made it clear to Sharpton that he embraced the values of "unconditional love, truth, the willingness to take abuse, to bear witness, and believe in the possibility of progress."

He told Sharpton that although he sympathized with black nationalism, and was friendly with such men as the Black Muslim Minister Louis Farrakhan, he was not a black nationalist.

"We argued back and forth," he said. "I'll never forget that meeting."

He said Sharpton told him that his meeting with West helped convince him to switch from his previous black nationalism stance to the positions of Jesse Jackson.

"Jesse comes out of the King legacy," West said, and that, apparently, was enough for him.

"People don't realize how brilliant he is," West said of Sharpton.

Of course, neither Sharpton nor West had any illusions that Sharpton could win the presidency. Their goal was to shake up the Democratic Party and try to move it from the more conservative stances it had been taking, starting in the Clinton administration, back to the more liberal party of Franklin D. Roosevelt, John F. Kennedy, and Lyndon B. Johnson.

"The Democratic Party has become more and more spineless," West said. "It has moved too far to the center. They're not talking about poor people as they should, the criminal justice system, affirmative action and full employment."

"We want to make sure the Democratic Party goes back to the New Deal and Great Society legacies."

The New Deal under Franklin D. Roosevelt and the Great Society under Lyndon B. Johnson were social programs

West's relationship with New York's outspoken Reverend Al Sharpton has been a ceaseless source of controversy. Nevertheless, West remains close with Sharpton, who is currently exploring the possibility of a presidential bid in 2004.

aimed at helping people in need. Some critics charge that in recent years, the party has moved away from such ideals.

Sharpton was ordained a Pentecostal Church minister at the age of 10. His favorite president was Lyndon B. Johnson, under whose administration the Civil Rights Act and the Voters Rights Act were adopted, providing for federal enforcement of the 14th and 15th Amendments for the first time.

Over the years, Sharpton made the New York City tabloid newspapers happy by becoming involved in a number of controversial issues. Probably the most sensational was the Tawana Brawley case.

Sharpton made himself the spokesman for Brawley, a black teenager who in 1987 claimed she had been raped by a gang of white men. The case dragged on for months, with charges and countercharges, and many glaring headlines. Finally, a grand jury concluded that her story was made up.

Sharpton told the Associated Press after his presidential announcement that he didn't think the Brawley case would hurt him.

"If that's all they got," he said, referring to his opponents, "I am proud."

Sharpton also served 90 days in federal prison for protesting the U.S. military bombing tests on the tiny Puerto Rican island of Vieques.

SLIPPERY SLOPE OF CHAOS

At a forum on National Public Radio in January 2003, West was asked how it was possible to get more white Americans to at least address the issue of "white skin privilege.

> We need to encourage our white brothers and sisters to speak more boldly. Again, it comes down to courage. They have to be willing to cut against the grain of their own respective communities.
>
> Bill Bradley was willing to do that. Ralph Nader was willing to do that. Al Sharpton's going to have to appeal to white brothers and sisters who are progressive, who are in some ways willing to engage in forms of self-critique that highlight their own white skin privilege.

And to the degree to which we can do that, we have some hope. If we can't, we just have to acknowledge maybe white America just doesn't have the capacity to deal with the depths of the white supremacist legacy. If that's the case, then we just slide down the slippery slope of chaos all together.

The history of American race relations was for many years marked by legal, cultural, and often violent methods of keeping black people down and out of power. In September 1862, President Abraham Lincoln issued an order to emancipate (free) the slaves held by owners in the Confederate States, the ones in rebellion against the Union. The final order was called the Emancipation Proclamation, issued January 1, 1863. Blacks celebrated it as the Day of Jubilee, and church bells rang throughout the North.

In December 1865, eight months after the Civil War ended, the 13th Amendment to the U.S. Constitution officially ended slavery throughout the country. But the end of slavery was only the beginning of black people's troubles in America, especially in the South where most of them lived.

Many Southern states adopted what were called "black codes." They were laws designed to keep blacks from many of the rights of white citizens. Some prohibited blacks from owning land, some imposed a nightly curfew for blacks, and some allowed states to jail blacks for not having jobs.

Congress took action to stop these laws. The Civil Rights Act of 1866 gave African Americans full rights as citizens, and the 14th and 15th Amendments to the Constitution further guaranteed the rights of blacks, including the right to vote.

The result was that some Southerners decided to make sure that blacks never enjoyed the benefits of these laws.

Between 1865 and 1866, approximately 5,000 blacks were murdered. Schools and churches were burned down. And more than 30 black citizens of New Orleans, Louisiana, were killed during a violent race riot in the city in 1866.

JIM CROW

The end of the Civil War marked the beginning of Southern whites' determination to keep blacks from voting or holding public office—or even to use the same rest rooms as whites. Segregated buses, trains, restaurants, theaters, schools, hotels, rest rooms, and even drinking fountains were established by state laws. These laws were called "Jim Crow" laws.

Thousands of black men were tortured and lynched by angry mobs of whites for various offenses, many of them false or imaginary. The idea was to keep the blacks terrified and "in their place."

The Ku Klux Klan, a secret society of racists, carried out violence against blacks. Klan members wearing hoods and robes rode through the countryside, attacking blacks and burning crosses as their symbol of hate. The Klan still exists today in various locations in the country, not all of them in the South.

A famous U.S. Supreme Court ruling in 1896 stated that there was nothing illegal about creating separate public facilities for blacks and whites—as long as they were equal. This became known as the "separate but equal" ruling. It never worked in practice. Black public facilities and schools were rarely equal to those of whites.

But even during those terrible times, some black leaders emerged in business, industry and the arts. There was Booker T. Washington, a former slave who became the founder of the Tuskegee Institute (now Tuskegee

University) in 1881. He urged blacks to stop trying for equality with whites and to seek to improve themselves economically. He advocated thrift and hard work.

George Washington Carver helped to revolutionize Southern agriculture by creating products from peanuts and other plants. Other accomplished blacks of the early 1900s included labor leader A. Philip Randolph, singer Paul Robeson, dancer Bill Robinson, who appeared in Shirley Temple movies, Olympic athlete Jesse Owens, and heavy-weight boxing champions Jack Johnson and Joe Louis.

In that same era, while blacks were being routinely murdered in the South, the Harlem section of New York City became a center of black arts and entertainment. The "Harlem Renaissance" featured a large outpouring of art, music and writing. Among the writers who gained fame— among whites as well as blacks—was the poet Langston Hughes. His work showed a strong identification with the black working class.

Another who came out of that creative period was the novelist Claude McKay, the first black literary figure of the 1920s to attract a large white audience. The novel, *Cane*, by Jean Toomer expressed the theme of the Renaissance in its identification with the black poor. Another poet who gained fame at that time was Countee Cullen.

In the theater, Eubie Blake and Noble Sissele produced a number of musical comedies featuring black performers. Black actor Charles Gilpin played more serious roles, includ-ing the title character in Eugene O'Neill's *The Emperor Jones*. Paul Robeson also performed in O'Neill's plays, as well as William Shakespeare's *Othello*, and the musical *Showboat*, in which he sang the famous song, "Old Man River."

In 1922, trumpeter Louis Armstrong went from New Orleans to Chicago to play with King Oliver's jazz band,

and Jelly Roll Morton began arranging jazz pieces that previously had been spontaneous. His work later inspired Duke Ellington and Fletcher Henderson.

Also in the 1920s, bandleader W.C. Handy composed "St. Louis Blues," making him known as the originator of recorded blues music.

THE LEGACY OF DU BOIS

One of the most significant efforts to bring blacks into the American mainstream began with W.E.B. Du Bois. He was born the year the 14th Amendment became law, in 1868, and died in 1963, the year John F. Kennedy was assassinated. In other words, he lived through an amazingly turbulent period of black history.

In 1905, Du Bois and other black leaders met in Niagara Falls, Canada, to discuss what could be done toward achieving civil rights for blacks. Out of the meeting came what was known as the Niagara Movement. From this movement, the National Association for the Advancement of Colored People (NAACP) was formed.

The NAACP concentrates its efforts on legal action, education, protests, and voter participation to reach its goals. In later years, black militants found this approach too timid and ineffective.

Du Bois was credited with reshaping black-white relations in America. He was the author of 17 books and numerous articles for many publications. He was not a great speaker, in the style of a Martin Luther King, Jr. His ideas were best expressed in his writings.

He advocated the creation of a "Talented Tenth" among black people. In other words, he felt that one-tenth of the black population could be educated and trained to be the leaders of the effort to pull up the other 90 percent.

In a critical essay about Du Bois in *The Cornel West Reader* (1999), West said he and Du Bois "are birds of very different feathers."

"My freestyle California spirit stands in stark contrast to his austere, New England soul."

West wrote that his own sensibilities were "rooted in gut-bucket blues and jazz," and violently clash with much of Du Bois' thinking.

"To put it bluntly," he wrote, "I am much closer—and proudly so—to the funk of a James Brown or George Clinton, the soul of a Curtis Mayfield, Richard Pryor, or Aretha Franklin, than he."

"Yet," he added, "we remain soul mates in our struggle for oppressed peoples, especially black humanity."

He called Du Bois the "towering black scholar of the 20th century." But he criticized Du Bois for what he called an inadequate interpretation of the human condition, and that he failed "to immerse himself fully in the cultural depths of black everyday life."

He quotes a passage from Du Bois in which he expresses horror and revulsion after attending a black revival meeting.

Du Bois wrote: "Those who have not thus witnessed the frenzy of a Negro revival in the untouched backwoods of the South can but dimly realize the religious feeling of the slave; as described, such scenes appear grotesque and funny, but as seen, they are awful."

West wrote that Du Bois' reaction to the black church service—not unlike those experienced by West himself in the Baptist churches of his childhood—"signifies for him both dread and fear, anxiety and disgust."

"It did so not simply because the folk seem so coarse and uncouth, but also because they are out of control, overpowered by something bigger than themselves," West wrote. "This clearly posed a threat to him."

"He certainly saw, analyzed, and empathized with black sadness, sorrow, and suffering," West went on. "But he didn't feel it in his bones deeply enough, nor was he intellectually open enough to position himself alongside the sorrowful, suffering, yet striving, ordinary black folk."

That idea of striving is very important to West. His position is that, yes, black people are suffering—just listen to the blues—but have not stopped striving and hoping for a better life.

That's what he hears in the blues, John Coltrane's music, and that of other black musicians and singers, not to mention R&B (rhythm and blues), hip-hop, and rap.

That's not always the hope that Du Bois expressed. After losing his 18-month-old son to diphtheria, he wrote this lament not only for himself but for all blacks suffering under the conditions that prevailed at his time of life:

"Within the Veil was he born, said I; and there within shall he live—a Negro and a Negro's son. Holding in that little head—ah, bitterly—the unbowed pride of a hunted race, clinging with that tiny dimpled hand—ah, wearily—to a hope not hopeless but unhopeful, and seeing with those bright wondering eyes that peer into my soul a land whose freedom is to us a mockery and whose liberty a lie."

About Du Bois' call for a Talented Tenth, West comments, ". . . He assumes that highbrow culture is inherently human-izing, and that exposure to and immersion in great works produce good people.

"Yet we have little reason to believe that people who delight in the works of geniuses like Mozart and Beethoven, or Goethe and Wordsworth, are any more or less humane than those who dance in the barnyards to the banjo plucking of nameless rural folk in Tennessee."

West, despite his great learning and his position as a teacher in some of the country's finest universities, never fails to identify with ordinary folk. He believes this is his advantage and strength over other academics who claim to know what the people want.

Referring again to Du Bois, West wrote, "As much as he hated white supremacy in America, he could never bring himself to identify intimately with the harsh words of the great performing artist Josephine Baker, who noted in response to the East St. Louis riot of July 1917, which left over 200 black people dead and over 6,000 homeless, 'The very idea of America makes me shake and tremble and gives me nightmares.'"

Josephine Baker (1906–75) was a black dancer and singer on Broadway in New York, who became fed up with the racial problem in America. She moved to France and became a French citizen.

Among those who stayed and fought was Ida B. Wells-Barnett (1862–1931), a fearless anti-lynching crusader and women's rights advocate. Like Rosa Parks many years later, she refused to give up her seat on a train to a white man in 1884 and was forcibly removed. She sued the railroad, losing the case in the Tennessee Supreme Court.

Another was Fannie Lou Hamer (1917–1977), who fought for the right of blacks to vote and suffered arrests and beatings by police. In 1964, she led the Mississippi Freedom Democratic Party delegation to the Democratic National Convention.

Some of the feelings about the black experience that Cornel West expresses were captured in August Wilson's famous play, *Ma Rainey's Black Bottom*. A character says, "As long as the colored man look to white folks for approval . . . then he ain't never gonna find out who he is and what he's about."

Another character says, "We done sold Africa for the price of tomatoes. We done sold ourselves to the white man in order to be like him."

7

Influential African-American Leaders

> "Malcolm X was the prophet of black rage primarily because of his great love for black people. His love was neither abstract nor ephemeral. Rather, it was a concrete connection with a degraded and devalued people in need of psychic conversion. This is why Malcolm X's articulation of black rage was not directed first and foremost at white America. Rather, Malcolm believed that if black people felt the love that motivated that rage, the love would produce a psychic conversion in black people; they would affirm themselves as human beings, no longer viewing their bodies, minds, and souls through white lenses, and believing themselves capable of taking control of their own destinies."
> —Cornel West, *Race Matters*

Cornel West was influenced by the black nationalist movement. This movement might be said to have started with Marcus Garvey. In the early years of the 20th century, some African Americans were coming to the conclusion that they were never going to receive fair treatment from the white establishment. They believed that they would be better off if they separated themselves from white society— or moved out of the country altogether.

Garvey was born in Jamaica on August 17, 1887, the youngest of 11 children born to Sarah and Marcus Garvey. His early activities were in Jamaica, where he organized workers to help better their condition. He founded the Universal Negro Improvement Association (UNIA) in Jamaica and later opened a branch in New York City. His message was that blacks should be separate from whites, and his enterprise was called the "black separatist" movement.

Garvey was a fiery speaker and liked to dress in military-style uniforms, complete with a plumed hat. He sat in an open car and led parades of his followers through the streets of Harlem. In 1921, he claimed his UNIA had one million members.

Garvey wanted blacks to free themselves from whites by establishing their own businesses. He started a steamship company, the Black Star Line, a newspaper, *Negro World*, and the Negro Factories Corporation to encourage black economic independence. Garvey was most famous, however, for his "back to Africa" campaign. He believed that blacks should leave the United States and return to Africa. That was what the steamship company was for, to take them there.

His dream didn't come true, however. The African nation of Liberia, founded by former American slaves, refused to admit him and his followers. His Black Star Line failed because of bad management. He was convicted of mail fraud, because of questionable stock transactions involving the company, and was sentenced to prison in 1925. He was pardoned by President Calvin Coolidge, and deported to Jamaica in 1927.

Garvey was called a dreamer by many, but he inspired pride in the mere fact of being black. He called himself "a proud black man, honored to be a black man, who would be nothing else in God's creation but a black man."

That boast appealed to many downtrodden African Americans suffering under the continued violence of the South and indifference of the North.

His rallying cry was, "Up, you mighty race! You can accomplish what you will!"

After his deportation, Garvey continued to work for black liberation in Jamaica and elsewhere. He died in London, England in 1940.

Garvey's work was a forerunner of the Black Power movement led by the Black Panthers and the Black Muslims in the 1960s. Their themes were similar—black pride and a distrust of the white power structure. A return to Africa was not part of their agenda, though.

As Cornel West writes in *The Cornel West Reader*, "Black nationalists usually call upon black people to close ranks, to distrust most whites (since the reliable whites are few and relatively powerless in the face of white supremacy), and to promote forms of black self-love, self-defense, and self-determination."

West says "a frightening sense of foreboding pervades much of black America today—a sense that fans and fuels black nationalism."

THE NATION OF ISLAM

Another influential black nationalist movement was initiated by the Nation of Islam, also called the Black Muslims. The Nation of Islam was founded in 1930 as the Lost-Found Nation of Islam by Fard Muhammad, also known as W.D. Fard. Elijah Muhammad, born Elijah Poole in Sandersville, Georgia, on October 10, 1897, became a disciple of Fard's. In 1932, Muhammad founded the Nation of Islam's Temple Number Two in Chicago, which became the largest mosque in the United States.

Fard mysteriously disappeared in 1934, and Elijah Muhammad took over the movement. Muhammad was so anti-white that he backed Japan in World War II because the Japanese are not white. He was jailed on a sedition (treason) charge as a result.

While in prison, he converted a number of fellow inmates to the Nation of Islam. Among the prison converts was Malcolm Little, serving a sentence for burglary. After his conversion to Islam, Malcolm Little became Malcolm X.

The Black Muslims considered Christianity to be the religion of the white oppressors who had kept blacks down. They despised white people. Muhammad called them "white devils." He promised his followers that African Americans, who the Black Muslims regarded as the original humans, would someday be restored to their rightful position as leaders of the world.

Whatever his failings, Muhammad is credited with building a strong, black religious group in the United States that appealed primarily to the unemployed and under-employed city dweller. Eventually, some members of the black middle class joined. He also contributed to the betterment of African Americans by establishing schools and businesses under the auspices of the Nation of Islam. Elijah Muhammad died in 1975.

Malcolm X had a powerful speaking style, in the manner of black preachers of old. He rallied many followers to the Nation of Islam. He was critical of the civil rights movement and opposed both integration and racial equality. He rejected all calls for brotherhood as being unlikely.

He called instead for black separation, black pride, and black self-dependence.

He stirred much controversy, such as when he said the assassination of John F. Kennedy was a case of the "chickens coming home to roost." By this, he meant that the violence used by whites was now being used *against* them.

After a pilgrimage to Mecca in Saudi Arabia (where the Islamic religion was founded in the 600s by the Prophet Muhammad), Malcolm moderated his views. He said he no longer believed whites to be evil, and agreed that there might be a chance for world brotherhood after all.

His change of heart angered some Black Muslim leaders. He was shot to death on February 21, 1965, while speaking at a rally in Harlem. Three Black Muslims were convicted of the murder.

LOUIS FARRAKHAN

Another influential Nation of Islam leader was Louis Farrakhan. Born on May 11, 1933, Farrakhan grew up in the Roxbury neighborhood of Boston. He was a talented youngster, and became a fine violinist. At the age of 21, in 1955, he went with a friend to hear Elijah Muhammad speak. Farrakhan liked what he heard and joined the Black Muslims shortly thereafter.

After Elijah Muhammad died, his son, Wallace Muhammad, took over. Wallace was much quieter and more moderate than was his father. He eased up on some of the movement's harsher attitudes toward whites. This approach didn't sit well with some Black Muslims, including Louis Farrakhan. In 1978, Farrakhan resigned from the movement and set up his own organization. He had many loyal followers.

In 1995, Farrakhan organized the Million Man March on Washington, D.C. Many people were surprised at the

In 1995, controversial Nation of Islam leader Minister Louis Farrakhan organized the Million Man March—a showing of solidarity among African-American men. Given Farrakhan's often-fiery rhetoric and anti-Semitic statements, many were surprised that the march was both well attended and peaceful. West remains friends with Farrakhan, though he does not share all of Farrakhan's views.

huge turnout, and that the outspoken Black Muslim minister could organize such a large, non-violent protest.

Farrakhan has been sharply criticized for his anti-Semitism. He has called Judaism a "gutter religion." And has made other nasty remarks about Jews.

Cornel West has made no secret of his friendship with Farrakhan. They have met numerous times. Both are prostate cancer survivors.

Rabbi Michael Lerner, also a good friend of West's, once called Farrakhan a "racist dog." Some have compared Farrakhan to Hitler and the Nazis, who killed six million Jews in World War II—or at least to the neo-Nazi skinheads, who advocate using violence against Jews. (The word "neo" means new. So the skinheads are "new Nazis.")

In *Cornel West: The Politics of Redemption*, Rosemary Cowan points out that West feels he must deal with Farrakhan because the Muslin leader represents a large group of followers whose voices must be heard in any discussion about race.

She quotes West as defending Farrakhan's attack on Judaism by saying, "What he meant was that Judaism has been used to justify various forms of domination. ...But we know that every religion has been used to justify domination."

He also doesn't think it's fair or accurate to compare Farrakhan to the Nazis. "Farrakhan says terrible things about the Jews," West said. "He does not advocate that people physically attack Jews."

West has always been opposed to anti-Semitism, as well as anti-gay attitudes. He has been particularly critical of the black church, which has been reluctant to condemn anti-gay behavior, because church leaders believe the Bible forbids homosexuality.

Cowan says West feels that Farrakhan "has a deep love for black people, but a limited vision of how to achieve black freedom."

Some of the conflict between Farrakhan and the Jews came to a head in 1994 when the NAACP held a National African-American Leadership Summit in Baltimore, Maryland. Both Farrakhan and West were invited.

Some Jewish leaders, including Michael Lerner, gathered outside the conference to protest Farrakhan's presence. West came out of the meeting and gave Lerner a hug. They had participated in many demonstrations and conferences together and were very fond of each other.

"West defended his presence at the summit on the grounds that the meeting's focus was on black suffering and pain, with the aim of generating strategies to 'address the state of siege ravaging much of black America,'" Cowan wrote.

Farrakhan's presence was as essential as West's since Farrakhan is "one noteworthy voice ... trying to understand and overcome pervasive black social misery."

"West believes he has a moral obligation to work with Farrakhan," Cowan wrote, "if the areas on which they agree can be used to build better communities and heal some of the deep divisions among African Americans."

One of West's problems is that he loves everybody. He is able to see through the attitudes and characteristics he might not like to where the humanity lies. We are all, as he frequently says, in the "funk" together, and are trying to get out in our own individual ways.

THE BLACK PANTHER PARTY

The Black Panther Party, founded in the late 1960s as the Black Panther Party for Self Defense, frightened everyone for a while with its cries of black power and hints that it didn't mind using violence to accomplish its aims.

In fact, several party members were killed by police in various clashes, and others were arrested for inciting riots and violence.

The organization was founded by Huey P. Newton and Bobby Seales in Oakland, California, in 1967, to patrol black neighborhoods and monitor police treatment of blacks.

Eldridge Cleaver, the party's minister of information, ran for president on the Peace and Freedom Party ticket in 1968. The Peace and Freedom Party was made up mostly of white activists opposed to the Vietnam War. Cleaver's running mate was Jerry Rubin, founder of the Youth International Party. Its members were called "Yippies."

The Black Panthers expanded nationwide and started programs that distributed food and health care to the needy, and built education centers in poor black communities.

But continual violent confrontations with police, FBI raids, and the arrest of group leaders finally put an end to the Black Panthers in the 1970s.

JESSE JACKSON

Jesse Jackson, a fiery speaker, had been a close associate of Martin Luther King, Jr., and had been at the motel in Memphis with King when King was shot to death.

Jesse Jackson was one of the most prominent black leaders in modern history. His work for racial justice actually began when he was a student at the North Carolina Agricultural and Technical College in Greensboro, North Carolina. He became student body president and encouraged the students to participate in sit-ins at segregated lunch counters. The well-publicized sit-in, by a group of black A&T students at Woolworth's segregated lunch counter in Greensboro in February 1960, set the tone for a series of similar sit-ins throughout the South that resulted in the integration of many restaurants.

In the mid-1960s, Jackson began working with Martin Luther King, Jr. in the Southern Christian Leadership Conference (SCLC), founded by King. In 1966, Jackson helped start the Chicago branch of Operation Breadbasket, the economic arm of the SCLC.

Jackson annoyed a lot of leaders of the SCLC, who accused him of using the organization for selfish purposes. He was expelled. But that didn't stop him. He founded Operation PUSH (People United to Save Humanity). He declared it would be a "rainbow coalition of blacks and whites gathered together to push for a greater share of economic and political power for all poor people in America." He later started the National Rainbow Coalition in Washington, D.C.

Jackson helped elect Harold Washington as the first black mayor of Chicago by uniting the black vote. He attracted huge crowds in South Africa, where he denounced the apartheid system in which blacks were kept apart from whites. He gave Palestinian leader Yasir Arafat a hug on a visit to the Middle East in 1979, touching off a controversy back home.

During his two campaigns for president—1984 and 1988—he gained an unexpectedly large number of votes. This made him a political force to be reckoned with. In 1984, he used his popularity in the Arab world to gain the release of Lieutenant Robert Goodman, who had been shot down over Lebanon. His work for the election of Bill Clinton in 1992 helped Clinton defeat then-President George H.W. Bush, the Republican incumbent and father of President George W. Bush.

Jackson has been accused of simply being a cheerleader for causes, a person who favors style over substance. Cornel West is among those who see Jackson that way.

West said Jackson's "presidential campaigns were the major progressive responses to (President Ronald) Reagan's conservative policies." But, he added, "Jackson's courageous leadership is problematic."

"His televisual style—a style too preoccupied with TV cameras—relies on personal charisma at the expense of grassroots organizing," West wrote in *The Cornel West Reader*. "His brilliance and energy sustain his public visibility at the expense of programmatic follow-through."

He added that Jackson's "televisual style may be reaching the point at which it undermines his crucial message."

Not everybody felt that way. President Clinton gave Jackson the Presidential Medal of Freedom in 2000. It is the nation's highest honor for a civilian.

But Jackson's image was damaged in 2001 when he admitted he had fathered a daughter, born in 1999, with a former staff member of his Rainbow Coalition. He has been married for more than 40 years to his wife, Jacqueline. They have five children.

HUMILITY AND LOVE

West strongly believes that Martin Luther King, Jr. was a breed apart from all the other black leaders before him.

"I always felt that they [other black leaders] lacked the self-critical moment of humility I discerned in the grand example of Martin Luther King, Jr.," West wrote in *The Cornel West Reader*.

"Such humility has always been a benchmark of genuine love for, and gratitude to, ordinary people whose lives one is seeking to enhance."

West compared King to the prophets of the Bible. "His all-embracing moral vision facilitated alliances and coalitions across racial, gender, class, and religious lines," West wrote of King. "His Gandhian method of nonviolent resistance highlighted forms of love, courage and discipline worthy of a compassionate prophet."

On August 28, 1963, King led a historic march on Washington, D.C., the largest civil rights demonstration in

West maintains an active schedule of speaking engagements, seeking to motivate social and political change. Here, West (second from left) walks to the podium during a February 2002 symposium on the future of African-American communities, held at the Sharon Baptist Church in Philadelphia.

history, with more than 250,000 in attendance. Standing on the steps of the Lincoln Memorial, he delivered his famous "I Have a Dream" speech:

> In a sense we have come to the nation's capital to cash a check. When the architects of our republic wrote the magnificent words of the Constitution and the Declaration of Independence, they were signing a promissory note to which every American was to fall heir. This note was a promise that all men would be guaranteed the inalienable rights of life, liberty, and the pursuit of happiness.
>
> It is obvious today that America has defaulted on this promissory note insofar as her citizens of color are concerned. Instead of honoring this sacred obligation, America has given the Negro people a bad check which has come back marked 'insufficient funds.'
>
> We must forever conduct our struggle on the high plain of dignity and discipline. We must not allow our creative protest to degenerate into physical violence.
>
> Go back to Mississippi, go back to Alabama, go back to Georgia, go back to Louisiana, go back to the slums and ghettoes of our Northern cities, knowing that somehow this situation can and will be changed. Let us not wallow in the valley of despair.

His long, passionate speech wound up with a series of "dreams" about the future possibilities of solidarity among races. Among them were:

> I have a dream that one day on the red hills of Georgia the sons of former slaves and the sons of

former slave owners will be able to sit down together at a table of brotherhood.

I have a dream that my four children will one day live in a nation where they will not be judged by the color of their skin but by the content of their character.

I have a dream that one day every valley shall be exalted, every hill and mountain shall be made low, the rough places will be made plain, and the crooked places will be made straight, and the glory of the Lord shall be revealed, and all flesh shall see it together.

He ended the speech, as he ended all of his speeches and sermons, with the words of an old spiritual: "Free at last! Free at last! Thank God almighty we are free at last!"

8

Songs of Hope

"Black culture consists of black modes of being-in-the-world obsessed with black sadness and sorrow, black agony and anguish, black heartache and heartbreak without fully succumbing to the numbing effects of such misery—to never allow such misery to have the last word. ... The black artists grapple with madness and melancholia, doom and death, terror and horror, individuality, and identity."

—Cornel West, *The Cornel West Reader*

John Coltrane's "Alabama" is heavy with sadness and despair. Listening to it, one cannot help thinking of the four little girls burned to death when their church in Birmingham, Alabama, was firebombed by the Ku Klux Klan in the 1960s.

Yet, Cornel West hears something else in the piece. "It's the saddest thing I ever heard," he said in an interview.

"There's a profound sadness and sorrow that deals with the hidden and concealed. And yet you hear a sense of possibility, of not allowing misery to have the last word.

"He takes you on a descent into the chamber of horrors. At the same time, he is saying we must keep our spirits up, keep fighting, don't succumb to hatred. Don't be taken into the gutter where they dragged you. Don't stay there."

The music of John Coltrane, the great tenor saxophonist, and many other jazz and blues musicians, have greatly influenced West's thinking. They have helped to shape his vision of the possibilities of America, the hope of better times ahead, especially for the oppressed and down-trodden.

In addition to "Alabama," West cites Louis Armstrong's "West End Blues," Duke Ellington's "Mood Indigo," and Sarah Vaughan's "Send In the Clowns" as a few of "the peaks of the black cultural iceberg."

He calls these songs "towering examples of soul-making and spiritual wrestling that crystallize the most powerful interpretations of the human condition in black life."

"This is why the black musical tradition in the 20th century is the most profound and poignant body of artistic work in our time," he writes in *The Cornel West Reader*.

He refers to Coltrane numerous times in his writings. He said in an interview that he sees Coltrane's "A Love Supreme" as "the greatest example of wedding the spirituality of the questioning spirit with service and praising. It contains a Socratic moment of self-questioning, and a prophetic deep compassion and reverence for God."

John Coltrane was born in Hamlet, North Carolina, on September 23, 1926. He lived most of his life in Philadelphia. He got much of his early musical experience with the jazz trumpeter Miles Davis, but also played with jazz great Thelonious Monk, before starting his own group. He died in 1967.

West traces black music to the spirituals sung from slave days onward. He grew up hearing these songs in the black churches of his childhood.

"As I grow older," he writes in *The Cornel West Reader*, "I find it more and more difficult to read the heart-piercing lyrics of the spirituals. They not only invoke precious memories of beloved family members and friends in those soul-stirring moments of my black church life; these songs also remind me of how difficult it is to engage in a deep-sea diving of the soul—a diving that may yield, if one is strong enough, bloodshot eyes and a tear-stained hope."

Like William Shakespeare's *Hamlet*, a man who yearns for revenge against the man who murdered his father, West says, "the spirituals are preoccupied with the memory of those beloved ones who have died and the desire for revenge against those who prosper from their evildoings.

"The major themes consist of mourning, suffering, resisting. Yet unlike Hamlet, who after much soul-searching commits murder, the heroes of the spirituals—namely, Jesus, Daniel, and Moses—triumph because they find great strength in an all-embracing love and mercy."

In her book, *Cornel West: The Politics of Redemption*, Rosemary Cowan describes West's view of blues music:

"The blues is written out of pain and keeps details of one's painful experiences alive, yet attempts to transcend the pain; it expresses the agony of life as well as the possibility of overcoming evil through endurance."

West often refers to a "blues sensibility" that he thinks should be injected into any discussion of race—the belief that in spite of past and present pain, people may endure and thrive with enough courage and perseverance.

Cowan quotes West as saying, "Profound music leads us—beyond language—to the dark roots of our scream and the celestial heights of our silence."

THE RAP ARTIST

Since West made his own CD, a blending of rap with narration and other forms of music, he has a special feeling for that brand of expression.

"The most important development in Afro-American popular music since 1979 is black rap music," he writes in *The Cornel West Reader.* "This music has been performed on ghetto streets and between stage acts during black concerts for many years."

The popularity of rap probably began with the release in 1979 of *Rapper's Delight,* by the Sugarhill Gang. Within months, West points out, black rap records were filling record shops around the country.

Black rap music is a "cry that that openly acknowledges and confronts the wave of personal cold-heartedness, criminal cruelty and existential hopelessness in the black ghettoes of Afro-America."

It is a cry, he says, of both "desperation and celebration of the black underclass and poor working class. ..."

He writes that some rap music challenges the vision of hope offered by the earlier forms of spirituals and blues.

"To put it bluntly," West writes, "the roots of the Afro-American spiritual-blues impulse are based on the supposition that somebody—God, Mom, or neighbors—cares. Some expressions of black rap music challenge this supposition."

His own album, *Sketches of My Culture,* was made to "try to communicate to young people, to reach out," he said in an interview. It also aimed to reach prisoners, the majority of whom are black or Hispanic.

"Some of the brothers can't read, but they love music," he said.

"Music is the last form of transcendence for many young people, to get distance from their pain," he added. "They don't read as much as I would like them to, but they can listen to this and get a lot of the same messages." (Transcendence, a word West uses a lot, means to go beyond the limits of ordinary experience.)

The CD was produced while West was still at Harvard University. It came out of a collaboration of his brother, Clifton, Michael Dailey, and producer Derek "D.O.A." Allen. They call themselves, "4 Black Men Who Mean Business."

In a review of the work in *Sojourners Magazine* (September/October 2001), Larry Bellinger wrote, "I listened to *Sketches of My Culture* over and over as its R&B riffs transported me to the '70s and its beats brought me to the realm of present day hip-hop."

The CD opens with "The Journey," which Bellinger describes as "a discourse by West on the evolution of music of the black experience in America. As West speaks, we first hear the shouts and guttural cries of the kidnapped in a foreign land, the rise of the spirituals into the tragic-comic perspective of the blues, and then on through jazz—"the finest art form of the 20th century, West says—R&B, and hip-hop—which fuses "linguistic virtuosity and rhythmic velocity."

The second track is called "N-Word." One critic said it "evokes the spirit if not the style of The Last Poets, a group whose song, 'Die, Nigga!' was about the negativity and self-hatred that comes from the self-identification of the word." It opens with a mock radio program over a soulful R&B groove. People call into the show to defend the use of the controversial word, and are quickly brushed off by the host, who wants to know why we use the word.

"The third caller is brother West, who, in his familiar lilting phrasing, says, 'We need a renaissance of self-respect . . . a renewal of self-regard . . . we ought not to use the word at all.'"

The next track, "Elevate Your View," has a heavy bass line under rap lyrics about love, life, and strife, interspersed with a hopeful message from West, who says "The past is prologue to your future."

A narrator addresses an inner city youth: "Excuse me, young brother. You over there with your pants sagging. Can I ask you a question? Are you familiar with 20-to-life? Or what about self destruction? Cause I've been watching you for a while, young man, the way you run around town with your gun in your hand, robbing, stealing maybe even killing, I got a bad feeling. So let me voice my opinion."

Then West's voice comes in: "Without self-respect you certainly self destruct. Be true to your history. Therein lies your possibilities. . . ."

The narrator comes back with: "Now check this out. I used to be just like you. Carrying a 9-millimeter just like you. Running around town with a knife in my shoe. On the corner shooting dice while I was drinking my brew. It's true. Until one day I got another view. A voice from upstairs, and you know who. Some spiritual guidance that dropped me a clue. Some guidance said you gotta love yourself before somebody love you."

The track called "The 3 Ms," extols the sacrifices of Martin Luther King, Jr., Malcolm X, and Medgar Evers. (Medgar Evers, who fought against segregation and racial discrimination in Jackson, Mississippi, was shot to death outside his home by a sniper on June 12, 1963.)

"Brother Martin, Brother Medgar, Brother Malcolm, we love you so. And miss you much. Your freely given blood fertilizes the tree of freedom. Your precious body ripped apart by the assassin's bullet sustains us in our struggle."

Then the chorus: "Martin, Medgar, and Malcolm, keep on keeping on, keep on staying strong. Martin, Medgar, and Malcolm, your work keeps living on, your spirit keeps us strong."

Of his CD, West wrote, "What you will experience here is an invitation to take an educational journey through the traditional African-American medium—music."

"A nourishing, inspirational story that must be told to every generation for fear of being forgotten and replaced with a 'safe' place of comfortable illusions. One that transcends legitimate bitterness and rage to arrive at an elevated place, where the view is clearer, and possibilities more attainable."

THE ACTOR

Cornel West, the movie actor, is another role this often surprising intellectual and scholar has sprung upon his friends and colleagues. In 2001, West got a call from Larry and Andy Wachowski, directors of *The Matrix*, who told him they had been influenced by his writings and wanted him in the sequels to their action-packed science fiction film.

A number of philosophers have pondered the themes of *The Matrix*—that the world has been taken over by a computer and humans are kept in cells where they supply energy to a vast computerized artificial intelligence. In the film, humans are tricked into believing they are living in reality.

William Irwin put together a book, *The Matrix and Philosophy*, a collection of the comments of various thinkers on the film. The questions the film raises concern the deep puzzles of what it means to be human, and what is life. The questions may be traced back to Rene Descartes, a French philosopher who lived from 1596 to 1650. He wondered if what we perceive as the world might be an illusion, perhaps created by a "malicious demon."

West said it was fun to fly to Sydney, Australia, for the filming of his role as Counselor West, a leader of the resistance. He was thrilled to meet Laurence Fishburne, Keanu Reeves, Carrie-Anne Moss, and the other stars of the films. He spent two and a half weeks filming.

"When they called me, I [West] told the Wachowski brothers that I could only do a role that has dignity." "They said, 'Oh, Dr. West, we wouldn't give you a role that didn't have dignity.'"

He said he spoke to the Wachowski brothers about philosophy and theology and other deep subjects. "Andy and Larry are really geniuses," he said. "These cats read a lot of philosophy. It's so rare. These cats are serious. I was just blessed to be there."

During an interview in August 2002 with *Washington Post* writer Lynne Duke, he produced photos of himself, swathed in yellow robes, awaiting makeup for his film shoot.

His eyes widened as he feigned the shock that would ensue when his critics saw him on the big screen: "This brother's in *The Matrix II* and *The Matrix III*? You got to be kidding!"

9

Justice Denied?

> "We are at a crucial crossroad in the history of this nation—and we either hang together by combating these forces that divide and degrade us or we hang separately. Do we have the intelligence, humor, imagination, courage, tolerance, love, respect, and will to meet the challenge? Time will tell. None of us alone can save the nation or world. But each of us can make a positive difference if we commit ourselves to do so."
>
> —Cornel West, *Race Matters*

On a cold, dark Philadelphia street on the early morning of December 9, 1981, Police Officer Daniel Faulkner was shot to death. When other police arrived they found a local radio journalist, named Mumia Abu-Jamal, seated nearby with a serious chest wound.

The police account of the shooting was that Abu-Jamal, working as a cab driver, saw Officer Faulkner involved in a struggle with Abu-Jamal's brother, William Cook, after a car stop at 13th and Locust Streets in the city's Center City neighborhood.

Police said Abu-Jamal rushed over, gun in hand, and shot Faulkner in the back. Faulkner spun around and fired at Abu-Jamal, striking him in the chest. Abu-Jamal then stood over the fallen officer and shot him again, in the head.

Three witnesses, who did not know one another, corroborated the police account. Two of them identified Abu-Jamal as the shooter. Two other witnesses said they heard Abu-Jamal boasting of shooting the officer while being treated at Thomas Jefferson University Hospital.

Abu-Jamal was convicted of murder, by a jury, at a hectic trial in which he refused to cooperate. He was sentenced to death.

That was the beginning of a case that has reverberated around the world as hundreds of people, from movie stars to ordinary people, rallied to Abu-Jamal's cause, proclaiming his innocence and demanding a new trial.

The primary argument was that Abu-Jamal was a victim of racism. Supporters of Abu-Jamal believed that he was being "railroaded" by a system that assumed that, because he was black and had spoken out against the Philadelphia criminal justice system, he had to be guilty. Family and loved ones of Faulkner, the 25-year-old decorated police officer, were just as loud in their demands that the jury's decision be carried out, and Abu-Jamal put to death for the murder.

High-powered defense attorneys filed numerous appeals, questioning the motives and accuracy of witnesses, and bringing up new information. There were numerous court hearings and rulings. There were rallies and demonstrations all over the globe. Meanwhile, Abu-Jamal remained in the death house. He spent his time writing books, and sending out commencement addresses on tape.

One of the supporters of Abu-Jamal was Cornel West. West wrote a foreword to one of Abu-Jamal's books, *Death Blossoms* (Litmus Books, 1996). The brief message expresses many of West's views of what it means to be black in America.

"The passionate and prophetic voice of Mumia Abu-Jamal challenges us to wrestle with the most distinctive feature of present-day America: the relative erosion of the systems of caring and nurturing," he wrote.

He went on to say that "this frightening reality, which renders more and more people unloved and unwanted, results from several fundamental processes." According to West, these include "the forces of our unregulated capitalist market, which have yielded not only immoral levels of wealth inequality and economic insecurity but also personal isolation and psychic disorientation."

He wrote that another factor is the "legacy of white supremacy," which, he says, "continues to produce new forms of geographical segregation, job ceilings and social tension."

"In short," he wrote, "our capitalist 'civilization' is killing our minds, bodies, and souls in the name of the American dream."

He expressed confidence that Abu-Jamal is innocent, and added that Abu-Jamal "speaks to us of the institutional injustice and spiritual impoverishment that permeates our culture. He reminds us of things most fellow citizens would rather deny, ignore, or evade."

THE PUNCTURED CEILING

Cornel West agrees that much progress has been made in race relations in recent years.

"Racial progress is undeniable in America," he wrote in *Race Matters*. "Never before have we had such colorful menageries of professionals in business, education, politics, sports, and the labor movement.

"Glass ceilings have been pierced—not smashed—by extraordinary persons of color. Overt forms of discrimination have been attacked and forced to become more covert."

The development of a new and prosperous black middle class constitutes "black progress alongside black working and poor communities that yield unprecedented increases in prison populations and overlooked victims of police abuse," he wrote.

"Decrepit schools, inadequate health care, unavailable child care, and too few jobs with a living wage set the stage for this social misery."

"The impact of the market culture," he went on, "has been devastating."

He points out that "50 years ago black communities were the most civilized and humane in America—highly nurturing, caring, loving, and self-respecting behind the walls of American apartheid.

"The market invasion, including the ugly drug invasion, has transformed too many black neighborhoods into hoods, black civic communities into black uncivil combat zones."

He notes that attractive black TV anchors and entertainment stars, as well as sports heroes, are not seen as threats by white Americans. It's the black man in the ghetto who strikes fear in their hearts.

West often uses the word "nihilism" to talk about attitudes in the black inner cities. Nihilism is defined as total rejection of beliefs in religion and morals.

"... The basic issue now facing black America [is] the nihilistic threat to its very existence."

West remains among today's most highly respected and visible African-American scholars. With many books—and a CD of spoken-word and rap material to his credit—he continues to reach new audiences with a message of strength, hope, and affecting change through compassionate political activism.

"This threat is not simply a matter of relative economic deprivation and political powerlessness—though economic well-being and political clout are requisites for meaningful black progress. It is primarily a question of speaking to the profound sense of psychological depression, personal worthlessness, and social despair so widespread in black America."

But West believes it is necessary to keep hope alive. He disagrees with Derrick Bell, author of *Faces at the Bottom of the Well*, who doesn't believe America will ever be anything but a racist society.

Rosemary Cowan, in *Cornel West: The Politics of Redemption*, says West believes that "the forces of evil can be pushed back." She wrote that the kind of hope that West keeps alive is "not a sunshine optimism, but rather a blood-drenched hope that his love-inspired struggle is not in vain."

Cowan wrote that West believes we must love America "for that in it which shows what it might become, as America needs citizens who love America enough to reimagine and remake it."

West's vision of a reimagined America is one that recognizes "the full humanity of all." He keeps on carrying on despite the racist incidents that have marred his life, and the actual dangers of violence he faces.

One day in May 1996, as he was preparing to leave from his home outside Boston to go to Salt Lake City to deliver the prestigious Tanner Lecture on Human Values at the University of Utah, a man in a ski mask walked up to the kitchen window and pointed a gun at his wife, Elleni.

The day before the lecture, organizers in Utah received an anonymous phone call telling them they might as well cancel the event because "Cornel West has been taken care of." He delivered the lecture under heavy security. The gunman was never identified.

"I am a threat," he said, "to the degree that I am trying to tell the truth about America."

But he sees himself as just a humble messenger, bringing a message of love, hope, and joy to the world. As he puts it in *The Cornel West Reader*, "I think that I'm just a brother who comes out of the black church on the block, trying to make sense of the world, and making a blow for freedom in the short time that I'm here—and having fun in the meantime."

1953: Born 2 June in Tulsa, Oklahoma, to Irene and Clifton L. West, Jr.

1957: Family moves to segregated neighborhood in Sacramento, California, called Glen Elder.

1963: Marches with parents in civil rights demonstration.

1963: Hears Dr. Martin Luther King, Jr. speak at Memorial Auditorium in Sacramento.

1966: Reads Soren Kierkegaard and decides to study philosophy.

1966: Reads about Theodore Roosevelt and decides to go to Harvard University.

1967: Family moves into a white neighborhood in Sacramento.

1967: Attends John F. Kennedy High School in Sacramento.

1967: Becomes president of student body and mediates racial problems.

1968: Dr. Martin Luther King, Jr. assassinated on 4 April, in Memphis, Tennessee.

1969: Graduates from high school.

1970: Enters Harvard University on scholarship.

1972: Arrested on false charges of rape; victim clears him of wrongdoing.

1973: Graduates *magna cum laude* from Harvard University.

1975: Receives master's degree and Ph.D. from Princeton University.

1975: Returns to Harvard University on a Du Bois Fellowship.

1977: Takes first teaching job at Union Theological Seminary, New York City.

1982: Teaches at Williams College in Massachusetts.

1984: Teaches at Yale University Divinity School.

1987: Arrested at Yale University in demonstration for clerical workers.

1987: Teaches for a semester at University of Paris.

1989: Becomes director of the Afro-American Studies program at Princeton University.

1993: Receives American Book Award for *Beyond Eurocentrism and Multiculturalism.*

1994: Returns to Harvard University as full professor in Afro-American Studies.

1994: Clifton West (Cornel's father) dies.

2000: Works on presidential campaigns of Bill Bradley and Ralph Nader.

2002: Advises Reverend Al Sharpton on presidential campaign.

2002: Has surgery for prostate cancer.

2002: Leaves Harvard University after dispute with new president, Lawrence Summers.

2002: Returns to Princeton University as professor of religion.

2002: Arrested in Washington, D.C., at demonstration on Israel-Palestine conflict.

2003: Appears as Counselor West in the sequel to the film *The Matrix, The Matrix Reloaded.*

Abu-Jamal, Mumia. *Death Blossoms*. Farmington, PA: Litmus Books, 1996.

Cowan, Rosemary. *Cornel West: The Politics of Redemption*. Malden, MA: Blackwell Publishers, 2003.

Du Bois, W.E.B. *The Souls of Black Folk*. Chicago: A.C. McClurg & Co, 1903.

Haley, Alex. *The Autobiography of Malcolm X*. New York: Random House, 1975.

West, Cornel. *Race Matters*. Boston: Beacon Press, 1993.

West, Cornel. *The Cornel West Reader*. New York: Basic Civitas Books, 1999.

Yancy, George. *Cornel West: A Critical Reader*. Malden, MA: Blackwell Publishers, 2001.

Further Reading

Bullard, Sara. *Free At Last: A History of the Civil Rights Movement and Those Who Died in the Struggle.* New York: Oxford University Press, 1993.

Haskins, James. *Freedom Rides.* New York: Hyperion, 1995.

Lucas, Eileen. *Civil Rights: The Long Struggle.* Berkeley Heights, NJ: Enslow, 1996.

McKissack, Patricia and Frederick. *The Civil Rights Movement in America From 1865 to the Present.* San Francisco: Children's Press, 1991.

Payton, Sheila. *African-Americans.* London: Cavendish, 1995.

Young, Andrew. *An Easy Burden: The Civil Rights Movement and the Transformation of America.* New York: HarperCollins, 1996.

Index

Index

Index

Picture Credits

page:

About the Author

John Morrison is a longtime Philadelphia newspaperman, freelance writer, and editor. He is the author of *Syria* and *Frida Kahlo*, both published by Chelsea House Publishers.